AF725822

Sunyana Sharma is a barrister at 3PB. She practises in health and safety, inquest and professional disciplinary law and has specialist knowledge in the areas of maritime and fisheries. She regularly represents the MCA, IFCA, masters, fisherman, companies and individuals as part of her maritime and fisheries practice and her cases have taken her as far as the Falkland Islands. She was called in 2006, is Head of the Inquest team at 3PB and is ranked in both Legal 500 and Chambers and Partners. She sits part time as an Assistant Coroner and Deputy District Judge.

A Practical Guide to Actions Brought by the Maritime and Coastguard Agency

A Practical Guide to Actions Brought by the Maritime and Coastguard Agency

Sunyana Sharma

Barrister, Inner Temple

LLM (Master of Laws)

Law Brief Publishing

© Sunyana Sharma

All rights reserved. No part of this publication may be reproduced, stored in a retrieval system, or transmitted, in any form or by any means, electronic, mechanical, photocopying, recording or otherwise, without the prior permission of the publisher.

Excerpts from judgments and statutes are Crown copyright. Any Crown Copyright material is reproduced with the permission of the Controller of OPSI and the King's Printer for Scotland. Some quotations may be licensed under the terms of the Open Government Licence (http://www.nationalarchives.gov.uk/doc/open-government-licence/version/3).

Cover image © iStockphoto.com/Thomas Faull

Internal diagrams © Rithika Sharma & Nishika Sharma

The information in this book was believed to be correct at the time of writing. All content is for information purposes only and is not intended as legal advice. No liability is accepted by either the publisher or author for any errors or omissions (whether negligent or not) that it may contain. Professional advice should always be obtained before applying any information to particular circumstances.

Published 2026 by Law Brief Publishing, an imprint of Law Brief Publishing Ltd
30 The Parks
Minehead
Somerset
TA24 8BT

www.lawbriefpublishing.com

Paperback: 978-1-918241-27-3

To my husband and girls,

who inspire me every single day…

PREFACE

When I was instructed in my first maritime collision case all those years ago, it was purely by chance. I had no connection to boats, the sea or anything maritime. Looking back, I remember there was very limited information on the subject. The law was difficult to digest and guidance on the subject was also minimal. The laws and regulations around maritime law may have become more accessible, however information is still scattered over many resources and finding the answers remains tricky to *navigate*. With this book, I wanted to create a comprehensive guide for the busy practitioner on actions brought by the MCA to help understand the basics of what is a ship, the responsibilities of masters, owners and seaman and the types of offences they can face, looking at the complete process from start to finish. As of 23 February 2026, the stated law in this book is up to date.

In producing this book, there are many people who I would like to thank. Jeremy Smart, the former Head of Enforcement, who gave me my first MCA case, Neil Cunningham who trusted me on many more MCA cases after that, Russell Kelly, Partner for LA Marine (retired), who instructed me to defend a young woman in a high profile and emotive MCA prosecution, which we won! HHJ Ian Lawrie KC who had so much faith in my abilities and Oliver Powell KC, a worthy opponent.

A very very special thanks to Simon Belfield, Partner at DWF Law, without his advice and input, this book would never been completed. My clerks, Russell Porter, Stuart Pringle, Dave Snook and Gemma Faulkner, I am eternally grateful to you all for getting me to this point and always having faith in me.

And finally to my beautiful and talented nieces, Rithika and Nishika who have produced the stunning pictures in the book, to both sets of parents and my wonderful husband, Ro, without whom I could never have achieved this. Your endless love, support and encouragement has kept me going even when I did not want to.

Sunyana Sharma
April 2026

CONTENTS

CHAPTER ONE

INTRODUCTION

Who are the Maritime and Coastguard Agency?

On 1 April 1998, The Maritime and Coastguard Agency ('MCA') was established when the UK Coastguard Agency and the UK Marine Safety Agency were merged. As an executive agency for the Department of Transport, the MCA today has two primary functions. These are:

i) as maritime safety regulator and

ii) as a 24-hour coastal and maritime search and rescue ('SAR') emergency coordination and response service for the United Kingdom[1].

This book will focus on the MCA's role as a safety regulator and look specifically at the actions the MCA can take in the courts, to enforce that role.

To understand what actions the MCA can bring it is necessary to understand the priorities of the MCA as a safety regulator. The MCA's motto is *'safer lives, safer ships, cleaner seas'*. To that end, its safety and environmental responsibilities extend to producing legislation and guidance on all maritime matters. Maritime standards are enforced through an inspection and survey regime by MCA inspectors and

1 *See* https://www.gov.uk/government/organisations/maritime-and-coastguard-agency/about.

surveyors which includes areas of vessel safety, security, pollution prevention and seafarer health, safety and welfare.

The MCA's Regulatory Compliance Investigations Team ('RCIT') are responsible for investigating suspected breaches of maritime legislation and determine what enforcement action should be brought.

The MCA is a unique organisation as it covers the entirety of the United Kingdom, i.e. England and Wales, Scotland and Northern Ireland. Its role extends to incidents anywhere in the world if it involves a British flagged vessel. The sinking of the Bayesian, a yacht, which sank off the coast of Sicily, tragically leading to the deaths of 4 people is one such example[2]. The MCA's duties are far more extensive than any other UK enforcement authority as their roles can be delegated to the devolved agencies.

Definitions

What is the sea?

The seas and ocean are vast. Each is interconnected, which means it is necessary to understand where one State may start and where another ends. So it can be difficult to understand who owns which part of the sea? The Law of the Seas was codified in the 1982 United Nations Convention of the Seas ('UNCLOS') and entered into force in 1994. It sets out a framework for the world's oceans, which defines maritime zones, regulates navigational rights and governs the management of

2 *See* https://www.bbc.co.uk/news/articles/c89g02dzkp3o.

resources. The main maritime zones as set out in UNCLOS are as follows[3]:

i) the **territorial sea** which extends 12 nautical miles from a sovereign state's coast line and is deemed part of that nation's sovereign territory. Foreign vessels have the right to navigate through this area, which is known as 'innocent passage';

ii) **Contiguous zone** extends a further 12 nautical miles from the territorial sea. Although navigation cannot be restricted in this area, a State can govern laws on four specific areas: immigration, taxation, custom and pollution;

iii) **Exclusive Economic Zones** (**'EEZ'**) is adjacent to the territorial seas and extends seaward 200 nautical miles from a state's coastal baseline. Under UNCLOS, in this area a coastal State has exclusive rights in relation to the natural resources in this area. An area can have an extended continental shelf of up to 350 nautical miles from the coastal baseline where a State has rights to the seabed;

iv) The area beyond the EEZ is known as the **High Seas** and/or international waters and do not belong to any State's jurisdiction.

3 *See* UNCLOS at https://www.un.org/depts/los/convention_agreements/texts/unclos/unclos_e.pdf

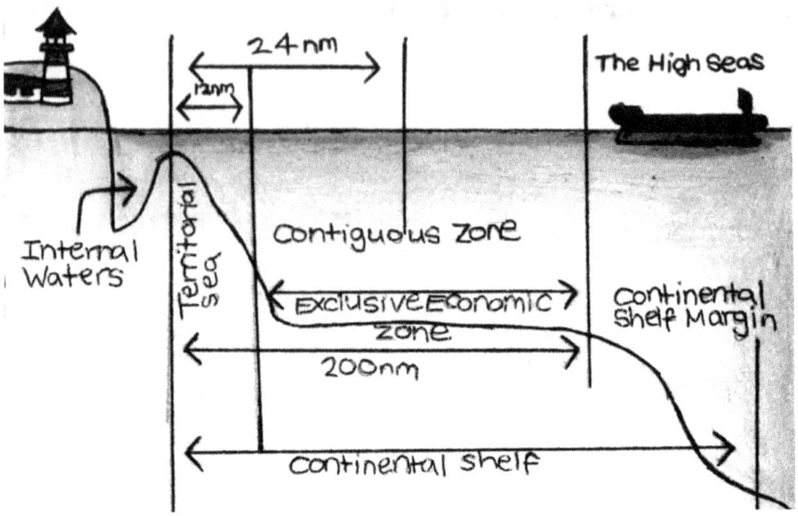

The International Laws and Conventions

A number of major international maritime conventions have been implemented into UK Law. A list of these key conventions is set out as follows with a brief summary of what they relate to:

a) *Article 12 of The International Convention of the High Seas 1958* renders a duty on the master of a ship to provide assistance to any person found at sea, assist in a rescue of persons at distress and after a collision render assistance to the other ship, her crew and her passengers. It also requires the establishment and maintenance of an effective search and rescue service regarding safety on and over the sea.

b) *Safety of Life at Sea ('SOLAS') 1974 and Protocol 1988* establishes a minimum safety standard for the construction, equipment and operation of merchant vessels. Flag States have the responsibility of ensuring that ships under their flag comply with the requirements under SOLAS.

c) *International Regulations for Preventing Collisions at Sea ('International COLREGs'), 1972*[4] is a convention designed to avoid collisions at sea. It recognises traffic separation schemes, deals with safe speed, rules concerning visibility, lights and sounds, the risk of collision, that action must be taken to avoid collisions and the conduct of vessels operating in or near traffic separation schemes, amongst other things.

d) *International Convention on Standards of training, certification and watch-keeping for Seafarers 1978 ('STCW')* sets out the minimum standards that States are required to meet for training, certification and watchkeeping for seafarers at the international level to keep seafarers safe at sea. These include but are not limited to the standards relating to masters, chief mates, officers in charge, navigational watches, seafarer deckhands, radio operators, all levels of engineers, radio operators and electro-technical officers.

e) *The International Convention on Maritime Search and Rescue 1979* is an international framework which sets out the responsibilities for maritime search and rescue. Under the Convention, States are required to have suitable arrangements in place for the provision of search and rescue services in their coastal waters. His Majesty's Coastguard ('HMCG') undertakes this role in the United Kingdom.

f) *Prevention of Pollution from Ships ('MARPOL') 1973 and Protocol 1978 ('Protocol 1978')* is the international

4 As amended by Resolutions A464(XII), A626(15), A678(16) and A736(18) of the International Maritime Organisation.

convention which prevents and minimises pollution from ships from both operational and/or accidental causes.

g) *Load Lines 1966 and Protocol of 1988* is an international safety convention which sets limitations on the draught to which a ship can be loaded to ensure a vessel can maintain adequate buoyancy and stability taking account of different zones and seasons. The 1988 Protocol harmonised the Convention's survey and certification requirements with those in the SOLAS and MARPOL Conventions.

h) *Maritime Labour Convention ('MLC') 2006* is a known as the 'seafarers' bill of rights' and establishes the rights of seafarers to decent work and living conditions including minimum requirements to work on ships, conditions of employment, accommodation, recreational facilities, food and catering, health protection, medical care, health and safety and accident prevention and complaint procedures for seafarers.

i) *International Convention on the control of harmful Anti-Fouling Systems on Ships ('AFS') 2001* requires parties to the Convention to prohibit and restrict the use of harmful anti fouling systems on ships which damage sea life and lead to harmful effects on the marine environment.

j) *International Safety Management ('ISM') Code adopted in 1993* sets out an international set of standards to support ship managers and companies to develop a safety management system ('SMS') to ensure the safe management and operation of ships and to enable pollution prevention.

What is a British ship?

Before considering what actions can be brought by the MCA, it is vital to understand what is a 'ship'.

Section 313(1) of The Merchant Shipping Act 1995 ('MSA 1995') provides that a ship *'includes every description of vessel used in navigation'*. In most cases, it will be obvious if a vessel is a ship however there will be those cases where the meaning of a ship will depend on the facts of the case. In *Clark (Inspector of Taxes) v Perks* [2001] EWCA Civ 1228 [2001] 2 Lloyd's Rep 431 [2001] STC 1254, a jack-up drilling rig with floating hull and retractable legs was held to be a ship. However in the case of *R v. Goodwin* [2005] EWCA Crim 3184, [2006] 2 All ER 519, [2006] 1 Lloyd's Rep. 432 a jet ski was not deemed to be a vessel used in navigation and therefore was not a ship under s.313(1) of MSA 1995. This has been confirmed in article 3 of the Merchant Shipping (Watercraft) Order 2023 ('Watercraft Order 2023') which provides that a watercraft is not defined as a ship or fishing vessel as per s.313(1) of MSA but is instead defined as any type of craft which:

a. is capable of moving under its own mechanical power,

b. is used, navigated or situated wholly or partly in or on water, and

c. is capable of being used to carry one or more persons.

As a result of the Watercraft Order 2023, the application of the 'dangerous use' provisions, such as the COLREGs and conduct endangering ships, structures or individuals under the MSA, now apply to watercrafts such as jet skis and other small leisure craft.

Historically, case law appears to suggest that when determining whether a vessel is used for navigation, the purpose for which a vessel is being used needs to be considered. Additionally, if the vessel has a rudder and is manned by a crew, these are important factors which are indicative of the vessel being a ship. However, the lack of these does not necessarily mean that a vessel is a ship[5].

Under Article 4 of The International Convention of the High Seas ('1958 Convention'), every State whether it is coastal or not, has the right to sail ships on the high seas under its flags. There is an expectation under the 1958 Convention that ships are to be registered with a country or State known as the 'flag state'. The requirements on a State who grants nationality to a ship are set out in Article 5 of the 1958 Convention.

The definition of 'British Ship' is provided for under s.1 of the MSA 1995. In essence a ship is British, if it is:

a. A ship registered in the United Kingdom under part II of MSA;

b. the ship is, as a Government ship, registered in the United Kingdom in pursuance of an Order in Council under section 308; or

c. the ship is registered under the law of a relevant British possession; or

---

5 The Mac (1882) 7 PD 126, 4 Asp MLC 555, CA; The Mudlark [1911] P 116; The Harlow [1922] P 175, 15 Asp MLC 498. The St Machar (1939) 65 Ll L Rep 119; Cook v Dredging and Construction Co Ltd [1958] 1 Lloyd's Rep 334.

d. the ship is a small ship other than a fishing vessel[6] and—

    (i) is not registered under Part II, but

    (ii) is wholly owned by qualified owners, and

    (iii) is not registered under the law of a country outside the United Kingdom.

e. A ship is a 'United Kingdom ship' for the purposes of the Merchant Shipping Act 1995 if the ship is registered in the United Kingdom under Part II of the 1995 Act and 'United Kingdom fishing vessel'[7] has a corresponding meaning.

A vessel that is registered as a British Ship is kept in a central register known as UK Ship Register[8]. The register is divided into four parts which are as follows:

a. Part I: commercial or pleasure boats, which are not fishing boats or registered as small ships under Pt III;

---

6 *See* MSA 1995, s.313(3): a 'fishing vessel' means a vessel for the time being used (or, in the context of an application for registration, intended to be used) for, or in connection with, fishing for sea fish other than a vessel used (or intended to be used) for fishing otherwise than for profit; and for these purposes, 'sea fish' includes shellfish, salmon and migratory trout, as defined by the Fisheries Act 1981 s 44 of the Fisheries Act 1981. However s. 313(3) confirms that a vessel for the time being used (or intended to be used) wholly for the purpose of conveying persons wishing to fish for pleasure is not a fishing vessel.

7 *See* MSA 1995 Part V.

8 *See* https://ukshipregister.co.uk/about-us.

b. Part II: fishing vessels;

c. Part III: small ships which are less than 24 metres long and which are pleasure boats; and

d. Part IV: bareboat charter ships.

When a seafaring vessel is registered in the UK, it is also allocated to a specific class. This will determine the use for which it is authorised, the certification it must hold and will set out what inspection and survey regimes it must adhere to. Any certification will depend on the type of vessel, size, nature of cargo and whether it is undertaking domestic or international voyages. The full list of certification requirements for merchant ships, passenger ships, small commercial vessels, large commercial vessels and fishing vessels can be found on the MCA website as they also operate the UK's shipping registry[9].

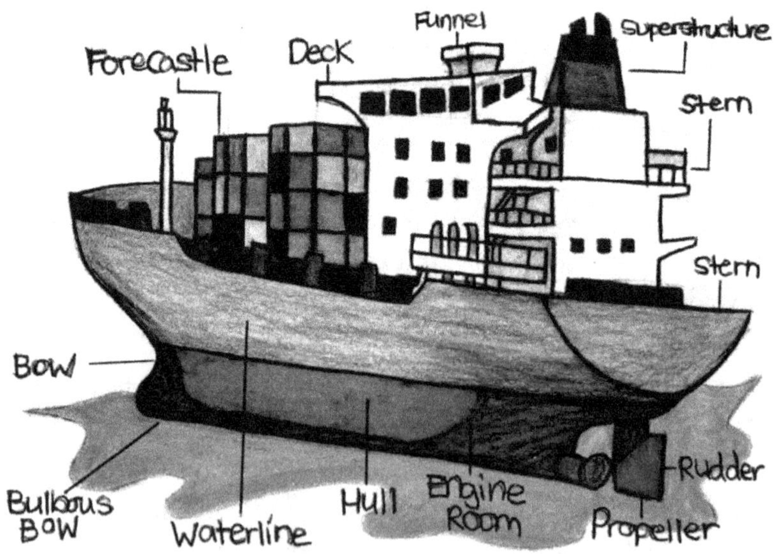

[9] *See* https://www.gov.uk/guidance/vessel-classification-and-certification#introduction

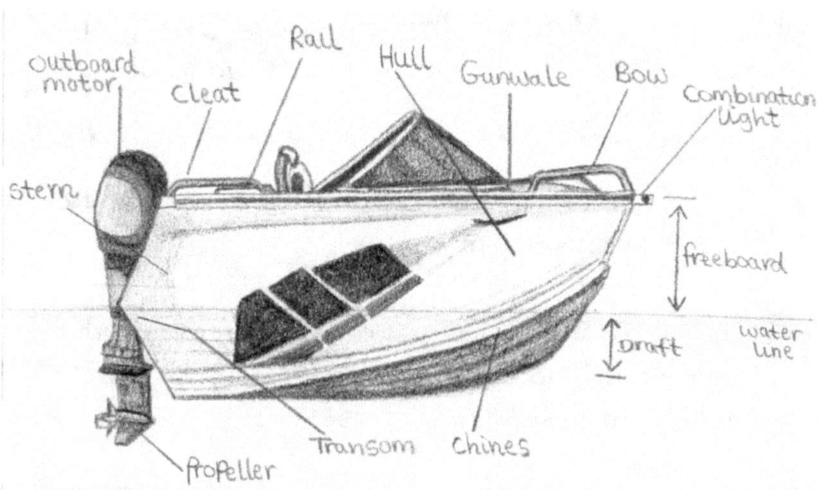
Outboard motor
Rail
Hull
Gunwale
Bow
Combination light
Cleat
Stern
freeboard
draft
water line
Transom
Chines
Propeller

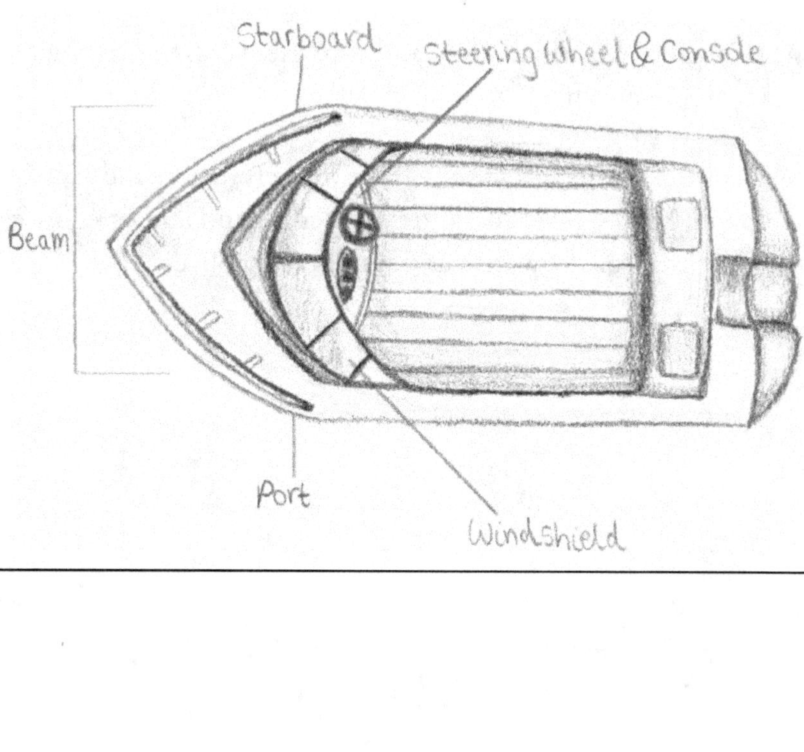
Starboard
Steering Wheel & Console
Beam
Port
Windshield

Categorisation of UK Waters

Waters in the UK not regarded as 'sea' in the MSA 1995 have been categorised in the Merchant Shipping Notice ('MSN') 1837 (M) Amendment 3[10]. This notice outlines four categories of water which are set out as follows:

- Category A: Narrow rivers and canals which have a depth of water of less than 1.5m;
- Category B: Wide rivers and canals where the depth of water is likely to be more than 1.5m and significant wave height is not likely to exceed 0.6m;
- Category C: Tidal rivers, estuaries and large deep lakes and lochs where the significant wave height is not likely to exceed 1.2m;
- Category D: Tidal rivers and estuaries where significant wave height is not likely to exceed 2m.

Annex 1 of this notice provides a table of each region and location of the England, Wales, Scotland and Norther Ireland and categorises the coastal and non-coastal waters as per the table above[11].

10 *See* MSN 1837 (M) Amendment 3: https://www.gov.uk/government/publications/msn-1837-m-amendment-3-categorisation-of-waters/msn-1837-m-amendment-3-categorisation-of-waters

11 *See* https://www.gov.uk/government/publications/msn-1837-m-amendment-3-categorisation-of-waters/annex-1

CHAPTER TWO

WHAT ACTIONS CAN BE BROUGHT BY THE MCA?

The ocean covers approximately 70% of the surface of the planet so it is unsurprising that a number of incidents can occur at sea. The most common issues that occur are as follows:

- Acts of pollution;
- Collisions;
- Unsafe operations leading to injury or death caused by hazardous operations like loading, unloading, mooring, working at height and/or exposure to toxic products;
- Conduct which endangers a master of its crew;
- Transportation of dangerous goods;
- Fraudulent seafarer documentation;
- Incidents aboard fishing vessels including vessels capsizing and health and safety incidents exposing crew to death or serious personal injury.

At present all enforcement action by the MCA is brought through the criminal courts with cases commencing in the Magistrates' Court. However, the MCA also has the power to issue enforcement notices such as improvement notices and prohibition notices. In November

2021, the MCA opened a consultation on an extension of their enforcement powers to include civil sanctions. At the time of writing this book, there has been no such extension to the MCA's powers. However in a later chapter, the possible civil sanctions envisaged by the MCA will be further explored.

Before the MCA can mount any prosecution, there are several considerations for the MCA before bringing an investigation. These are as follows:

1. Do they have jurisdiction to investigate/prosecute?

2. Who do they investigate?

3. Should they investigate?

4. When can they prosecute?

Do they have jurisdiction to prosecute?

Alongside the Crown prosecution Service, there are a number of alternative enforcement agencies including the Health and Safety Executive ('HSE'), Local Authorities, the Serious Fraud Office, National Crime Agency, Financial Conduct Agency, the Environment Agency and His Majesty's Revenue and Customs to name but a few. In most cases it will be obvious who the prosecuting authority is.

The MCA is lesser known as an enforcement agency. The powers and responsibilities of the MCA derive from the MSA 1995, Coastguard Act 1925 and the Merchant Shipping and Maritime Security Act 1997.

The RCIT[12] acts as both investigator and prosecutor of maritime offences. Their jurisdiction extends to marine offences for breaches under the MSA 1995 and associated regulations such as, but not limited to, the Merchant Shipping (Management Code) Regulations 2014 and the Merchant Shipping (Distress Signals and Prevention of Collisions) Regulations 1996. The MCA's jurisdiction to prosecute applies to United Kingdom Ships anywhere in the world and any other ship navigating within the UK and its territorial waters. Therefore, the MCA's power to prosecute can extend to a British national in a foreign port and foreign nationals onboard a British Ship on the High Seas.

Collaboration with other Agencies

Although the MCA are the primary authority which enforces maritime regulations and laws, it works very closely collaborating with other agencies such as the Police, Marine Policing Unit ('MPU)[13], HSE, EA, Marine Management Organisation ('MMO')[14] and Harbour Authorities when investigating criminal activity on or around the water.

The MCA is party to an agreement with the CPS and other prosecution agencies known as the Prosecutors' Convention 2009[15].

12 Once known as the MCA's Enforcement Unit.

13 The MPU river police along the River Thames based at Wapping Police Station and are responsible for 47 miles of the River Thames between Dartford and Hampton Court.

14 The MMO was created under the Marine and Coastal Access Act 2009 and protect and enhance the marine environment.

15 *See* The Prosectors' Convention 2009: https://www.cps.gov.uk/publication/prosecutors-conventions-2009.

The purpose of the Convention is to set out the responsibilities of prosecutors when one or more authority and/or investigating body share power to take action to ensure that cases are dealt with justly and serve the public interest. Agencies are obligated to work together in a co-ordinated fashion so that decisions are made promptly, to actively manage communications and interactions with other investigators and prosectors at the earliest possible opportunity and to enforce the law effectively and fairly.

The MCA is a signatory alongside a number of enforcement agencies to the Work-Related Deaths: A Protocol for Liaison' ('WRDP') in England and Wales[16] and the WRDP in Scotland ('WRDP Scot')[17]. These protocols apply to fatalities that have resulted from or are in connection with work.

These protocols are a guide to ensuring effective joint work-related investigations between the various agencies. The WRDP makes clear that *'only the police can investigate homicide related offences (corporate or gross negligence manslaughter), and only the CPS can decide whether a case can proceed.'*[18] Therefore although the Police have primacy for an investigation when there are suspicions of a negligent homicide, they will continue to work jointly with any other relevant enforcing authorities. Following the death of four paddleboarders in Haverford West, Pembrokeshire in October 2021, the CPS and HSE led a joint investigation into the tragic deaths of the four individuals. The joint investigation led to a gross negligence manslaughter conviction of the

---

16 *See* https://www.hse.gov.uk/pubns/wrdp1.pdf for WDRP England and Wales (last updated in September 2011)

17 *See* https://www.copfs.gov.uk/publications/work-related-deaths-a-protocol-for-liaison/html/ WRDP for Scotland (last updated on 8 May 2025).

18 *See* para 2.4 of WRDP.

paddleboard firm owner alongside a breach under the Health and Safety at Work Act 1974 in March 2025[19].

The WDRP makes clear that the MCA's responsibility extends to *'enforcing work-related health and safety legislation aboard commercial vessels of any size and in the case of UK vessels this applies to anywhere in the world and in the case of other vessels whilst they are in UK waters.'*[20]

The MCA and the Marine Accident Investigation Bureau ('MAIB')[21]

The MAIB is a marine safety investigator which sits as an independent unit within the DfT. It is responsible for investigating accidents related to ships and crew to determine the causes of accidents at sea. Within their reports the MAIB seek to provide recommendations on safety improvements and increase awareness of how accidents occur. Their powers derive from s.267 of the MSA 1995 and The Merchant Shipping (Accident Reporting and Investigation) Regulations 2012[22], which defines when an accident and/or incident may be investigated, the requirements for reporting accidents and for publishing reports. Therefore, the sole objective[23] of the MAIB is to prevent future death

---

19 *See* https://press.hse.gov.uk/2025/04/23/paddleboard-tour-leader-jailed-over-deaths-of-four-people/.

20 *See* p.10 of WRDP.

21 See MAIB website at: *https://www.gov.uk/government/organisations/marine-accident-investigation-branch*.

22 Updated by The Merchant Shipping (Accident Reporting and Investigation) and the Railways (Accident Investigation and Reporting) (Amendment) (EU Exit) Regulations 2018.

23 See Regulation 5 of The Merchant Shipping (Accident Reporting and Investigation) Regulations 2012.

by ascertaining the cause and circumstances of an accident. The investigation does not determine liability or apportion blame.

As the respective roles of the MCA and MAIB differ, it is important to note that an MAIB report cannot form any part of an MCA prosecution given that its ultimate purpose is to prevent future death. This is because the MAIB report is not written with litigation in mind and, pursuant to Regulation 14(14) of the Merchant Shipping (Accident Reporting and Investigation) Regulations 2012, it shall be '*inadmissible in any judicial proceedings whose purpose, or one of whose purposes is to attribute or apportion liability or blame*'.

A Memorandum of Understanding ('MOU') between HSE, MAIB and MCA

The MCA has entered into a joint MOU with both the HSE and MAIB to ensure collaborative working between these organisations where there is an overlap between health and safety enforcement and accident investigations at the water margin, offshore and on inland waterways in and around the UK. Due to the cross over between these jurisdictions, an Operational Working Agreement ('OWA')[24] has been put in place between all three organisations. This identifies the lead enforcement and/or investigation authority for a given activity.

Given the specific safety role of the MAIB and the importance placed on safety considerations, the MAIB investigation often runs parallel to the MCA/HSE enforcement investigations and may, at times, take

24 *See* OWA at: https://www.gov.uk/government/publications/memorandum-of-understanding-between-mca-hse-and-maib/operational-working-agreement-between-mca-hse-and-maib#fnref:2.

precedence over a criminal investigation, if it is in the public interest for it to do so.

The OWA confirms that jurisdiction between the differing organisations is divided as follows:

- HSE: Work activities covered by Health and Safety at Work Act etc. 1974 ('HSWA') and relevant statutory provisions, e.g. docks, jetties, loading, cargo operations, ship repair, offshore installations[25], energy structures, wells and pipelines, aquaculture.

- MCA: UK ships and those working on them anywhere in the world, foreign flag ships and those working on them in UK waters, search and rescue co-ordination in UK SAR.

- MAIB: all marine incidents/accidents in the territorial sea and on inland waterways, incidents/accidents involving UK ships anywhere in the world and investigation of a foreign vessel outside the territorial sea when no UK flagged vessel is involved if directed by the Secretary of State to do so.

In essence the MCA takes the lead for enforcement on any normal ship activity under the control of the master of a UK vessel anywhere in the world so long as it is not an offshore installation or energy structure. However, if a vessel is involved in an activity connected to an offshore installation undertaking oil and gas exploration or production, underground coal gasification or gas storage and

25 Offshore installation" means fixed or floating platform, including drilling rigs, floating production storage and offloading facilities used for the offshore production and storage of oil, and floating storage units used for the offshore storage of produced oil.

importation, energy structure, or is in a dock or a harbour area *and*[26] the activity is under the control of the Master, then the MCA continue to be the lead authority.

The MCA will not lead on an activity performed by a non-UK flagged vessel in the UK continental shelf. In this scenario, the lead authority would be the HSE if the activity is one that falls under the HSWA. For any other activity, the Flag State would take the lead. However, the MCA will remain the lead enforcement agency for non-HSWA activity which is not under the control of the master of the vessel on a UK vessel anywhere in the world or a non-UK flagged vessel in the territorial sea.

One of the most difficult areas to assess is who has the jurisdiction and where that jurisdiction overlaps in respect of incidents and fatalities involving vessels and offshore oil, gas and renewal energy installations. The OWA provides further guidance on the many possible scenarios such as mobile installations in transit and whether they meet the definition of a vessel. However, the question of whether the HSE or MCA are the lead enforcement agency will very much depend on the specific nature of the incident.

Other regulators

In general the MCA normally take the enforcement lead for issues relating to navigation, vessel standards such as stability and crew competence on commercial vessels. Many of maritime regulations relate to specific classes of vessel that operate commercially in certain categorised waters. However, given the definition of *'ship'* as *'any vessel used in navigation'* in the MSA 1995, the power of the MCA extends to inland waters. It is therefore important to note that the MCA often

---

26 Emphasis added.

work with other regulators on vessel related issues such as Local Authorities, Adventure Activities Licensing Authority ('AALA')[27] and Port and Harbour Authorities.

In addition, each harbour and/or authority will have its own set of local laws known as bye-laws, which deal with the administration and regulation of the specific harbour and/or authority concerned on matters such as navigation, mooring, launching, vessel traffic and handling of goods and cargo. Any regulatory breaches of bye laws are therefore enforced by the harbour or port authority concerned, through the criminal courts.

The 2025 Port and Marine Facilities Safety Code ('Port Code') provides a set of national standards and guidance for all ports, harbours, marine facilities, berths and terminals in every aspect of marine facility safety. The Port Code was originally introduced in 2000 following the grounding of the Sea Empress at Milford Haven, Wales in 1996 which led to a major oil spill. The aim of the Port Code is to establish the duties relating to the safety of those working in and/or using harbours, ports, marinas and their facilities. Compliance with the Code is not mandatory however the legal duties are good practice and recognised by the industry. The duties within the Port Code arise from the Harbours Act 1964, Dangerous Vessels Act 1985, Pilotage Act 1987 and MSA 1995. The MCA advises DfT on the application of the code to all organisations in the UK and provides advice and assistance on compliance. It is therefore unsurprising that if a marine accident or incident were to occur within a harbour or authority, it is likely to collectively engage the MCA, MAIB and HSE.

27 AALA is responsible for licensing adventure activities. Further details can be found here: https://www.hse.gov.uk/aala/licensing-authority.htm.

CHAPTER THREE

OFFENCES, PROSECUTION AND SENTENCE

When is a Criminal investigation likely to follow?

The MCA's approach to investigations and prosecutions are set out in the MCA enforcement policy statement[28].

Under s.256(1) of MSA 1995, the Secretary of State has appointed a team of inspectors and surveyors to support the enforcement role of the MCA. The RCIT are the delegated team that have the responsibility to investigate any suspected breaches of maritime legislation that may impact on the safety and security of individuals, vessels, and the environment. A criminal investigation will commence if there has been 'significant breach' of the legislation such as where there has been or has the potential to cause loss of life, serious personal injury, significant pollution or damage to property of the environment. The RCIT will also investigate obstruction offences and instances of persistent non-compliance or if the MCA deem there to be a public interest to investigate a case.

The MCA defines 'significant breach' as:

---

28 *See* MCA Enforcement Policy Statement: https://www.gov.uk/government/publications/mca-enforcement-policy-statement/mca-enforcement-policy-statement#:~:text=with%20the%20Court.-,2.,carrying%20out%20their%20statutory%20functions.

- *'contravention of legislation appertaining to ships, watercraft, seafarers, or other water users, which has, or has the potential to cause, loss of life, serious injury, significant pollution or damage to property or the environment.*

- *an act which prevents an officer of the MCA from carrying out their statutory functions.'*

Before the MCA decide to prosecute, a recommendation is made by the MCA Departmental Inspector. This decision is reviewed independently in accordance with the Code for Crown Prosecutors. The final decision to prosecute is then made by the MCA Chief Executive or delegated to an Executive Director.

It is important to be aware that the MCA may also investigate incidents or breaches that do not reach the 'significant breach' criteria if they consider it appropriate to do so.

As with the CPS and HSE, the MCA will not instigate a prosecution unless it meets the Full Code test as set out in the Code for Crown Prosecutors[29]. Therefore, the MCA must apply the following two stage test before embarking on any prosecution:

1. **Evidential stage:** it is satisfied that there is sufficient evidence to provide a realistic prospect of conviction in respect of each suspect on each charge and that this evidence is admissible, reliable and credible;

2. **Public interest stage:** it will also consider if the decision to prosecute is in the public interest.

[29] *See* The Code for Crown Prosecutors: https://www.cps.gov.uk/publication/code-crown-prosecutors

The list of questions that the MCA will consider when determining the public interest relate to the seriousness of the offence, the level of culpability, the harm caused, the age and maturity of the suspect, the impact of the offence on the community, whether a prosecution is a proportionate response and whether sources of information require protection.

Who to prosecute

There are a number of possible offenders that the MCA may prosecute. They will either be an individual, corporate entity or company. The individuals most often prosecuted by the MCA are the master of the vessel. A master is defined as *'every person (except a pilot) having command or charge of a ship and, in relation to a fishing vessel, means the skipper'*.[30] It is well known in law that a master owes a duty of care to all those who sail on a vessel. However, offences can also be committed by seamen, who are *'every person (except masters and pilots) employed or engaged in any capacity on board any ship'*[31]. The definition of a seaman is therefore drawn purposely wide to capture all other officers on a ship. Offences relating to a seaman normally arise from non-compliance with maritime obligations when operating the vessel.

A pilot is excluded from the definitions above as their roles are specific to guiding and navigating ships safely through hazardous areas such as narrow channels or ports. The definition of a pilot is set out at s.31 of Pilotage Act 1967 and *'means any person not belonging to a ship who has the conduct thereof and "pilotage" shall be construed accordingly'*.

30 *See* s.313(1) of the MSA 1995.

31 *See* above.

In addition to the master, owners of vessels can also be prosecuted whether they are individuals or corporate entities for breaches of maritime legislation. Such offences largely relate to unsafe operations and/or a dangerously unsafe ship. Owners can also be liable for discharge of pollution from a vessel.

Following the implementation of the International Safety Management Code, which has been formalised in the Merchant Shipping (International Safety Management (ISM) Code) Regulations 2014 ('ISM Code Regulations 2014') and the Corporate Manslaughter and Corporate Homicide Act 2007, corporations are not only liable for the actions of the master, but also for the actions of any of the crew members who have a management role. Under the ISM Code Regulations 2014, an ISM Company is a either the owner of a ship or it is a person who is not the owner of the ship but who '*has assumed responsibility for the operation of the ship and has agreed with the owner to take over all the duties and responsibilities imposed by the ISM Code, that person.*'[32]

Officers of a body corporate can also be subject to a prosecution according to section 277 of MSA 1995. An officer within the corporation such as a director, manager, secretary or other similar officer who acts in that capacity will be prosecuted, alongside the body corporate, if an offence is proved to be committed with their consent, connivance or if neglect can be attributed to them. The term 'officer' can therefore be widely interpreted by the Courts.

Due to the considerable management and costs involved in operating a vessel, it is not uncommon for vessels to be hired out to a charterer and/or for owners of a vessel to contract out the safety management of the ship to another. Therefore for some offences, such as s.98 and 100 of the MSA, the legislation recognises that ships can be chartered by

---

32 *See* regulation 2.

demise or managed wholly or in part by another person other than the owner. Therefore an entity who manages or charters a vessel can be prosecuted alongside individuals or even the owner depending on the facts and circumstances of a case. In such a case the management or Barebone Charter Party Agreement will need to be carefully reviewed to ascertain the extent of the responsibilities of those involved in operating a vessel.

Offences to Prosecute

The MCA enforcement policy statement[33] confirms that the offences brought by the MCA are largely divided into the six following groups:

a. Pollution

b. Breaches of collision regulations

c. Unsafe operations – owners, operators and users

d. Conduct endangering masters and crew

e. Carriage of dangerous goods

f. Fraudulent completion of seafarer documentation.

The offences for each category can be found in the MSA and/or associated regulations. Although there are a number of offences for which the MCA can and does prosecute, it would be impossible to deal with each and every maritime breach in this chapter. To that end, a selection of offences has been chosen across each group of offences

---

33 *See* paragraph 4.

and outside the group to give the reader an understanding of the obligations that can attach to ships, their owners, masters and seamen.

Pollution

Section 128 of MSA gives effect to the international agreements governing the prevention of pollution by ships. In essence offences range from discharging of pollution such as garbage and oil from ships to the failure to report incidents involving pollution or the threat of pollution. Consequently, there are numerous pollution offences that the MCA regulate such as:

Discharge of oil from ships:

Under s.131 of MSA, it is a criminal offence to discharge oil or a mixture containing oil from a ship which is 1) an offshore installation and into UK national waters which are navigable by sea going ships or 2) from a ship which is not an offshore installation and into UK national waters which are navigable by sea going ships which do not form part of the sea. Sea in this context includes any estuary or arm of the sea. An owner or master guilty of such an offence is liable on summary conviction to a fine not exceeding £250,000 and on a conviction on indictment to an unlimited fine.

The Merchant Shipping (Prevention of Oil Pollution) Regulations 2019 ('The Prevention of Oil Pollution Regulations'):

The Prevention of Oil[34] Pollution Regulations implement Annex I of MARPOL. They also have ambulatory effect and therefore any amendments or changes to the international convention under MARPOL and the Polar Code will automatically be applied and incorporated into these regulations[35]. The Regulations apply to UK ships and non-UK ships within UK waters subject to certain exceptions[36]. Under these regulations a survey, certification and oil record book regime[37] is required before a ship can proceed or attempt to proceed at sea. There are two types of certificates under the regulations: the IOPP certificate which is the International Oil Pollution Prevention Certificate issued in accordance with regulation 7 of Annex I and the UKOPP Certificate which is the United Kingdom Oil Pollution Prevention Certificate issued by the MCA in accordance with the Merchant Shipping (Prevention of Oil Pollution) Regulations 2019.

---

34 Oil is defined in regulation 1, Annex I of MARPOL as: 'petroleum in any form including crude oil, fuel oil, sludge, oil refuse and refined products (other than those petrochemicals which are subject to the provisions of Annex II of the present Convention) and, without limiting the generality of the foregoing, includes the substances listed in appendix I to this Annex'

35 The Merchant Shipping (Prevention of Oil Pollution) Regulations 2019, regulation 4.

36 *See above,* regulation 5.

37 *See above*, regulations 6, 7, 10, 12, 13 and 20.

This applies to oil tankers which have 150 or more gross tonnage and UK ships which are not oil tankers but have a gross tonnage of 400 or above.

There are also technical requirements relating to the condition and equipment of the ship and on board equipment as prescribed under Annex I of MARPOL to ensure the ship does not proceed to sea presenting an unreasonable threat of harm to the marine environment.[38] These relate to the construction, provision of equipment and operation of the machinery space under part 4 and similar provisions in respect of cargo areas in part 5. Such a responsibility befalls on the owner and master of a ship and any accident or defect discovered to a ship must be reported to the Certifying Authority at the earliest opportunity if such accident or defect *'substantially affects the integrity of the ship or the efficiency or completeness of the equipment of the ship'* under the regulations[39]. In such circumstances, the Certifying Authority such as the MCA will carry out an investigation to determine any necessary repairs or whether an additional survey is required. If a ship is deficient and it or its equipment does not correspond with the relevant certificate issues or condition or the ship is unfit to proceed to sea without presenting an unreasonable threat of harm to the marine environment, the MCA can require corrective action to be taken. If such corrective action advised by a surveyor is not taken within a specified time, by an owner and master of a vessel, the IOPP or UKOPP Certificate can be withdrawn[40].

Part 3 of the Prevention of Oil Pollution Regulations prohibits the discharge of sea oil or oily mixtures into the sea from certain ships or

38 *See above,* regulation 11.

39 *See above,* regulation 11(3).

40 *See above,* regulation 17.

oil tankers with some exceptions[41]. Under regulation 34, ships are also required to carry on board a shipboard oil pollution emergency plan. To ensure compliance with these Regulations, inspectors have powers to inspect the ship and its equipment under regulation 36. Such powers may be exercised if the ship is in a UK port or is at an offshore installation in UK waters or controlled waters.

Any contravention of the Prevention of Oil Pollution Regulations is deemed to be a criminal offence by the owner and master under regulation 42. Offences include but are not limited to proceeding to sea without a valid IOPP or UKOPP Certificate (regulation 6), failing to comply with the master and owner's responsibilities of a UK ship (regulation 11, 16(2) or (4), 19, 34, 35), discharging oil when prohibited to do so (regulations 25 to 28A) and failing to comply with the technical requirements relating to the condition and equipment of the ship and on board equipment (regulations 29 to 33). Offences can be committed by the owner, manager and demise charterer alongside the master of the ship. Offences are punishable by fine both on summary conviction and conviction on indictment.

41 *See above,* regulations 21 to 28A.

Further guidance is provided in MGN 603(M) Requirements for Oil or Oily Mixture Discharges for Offshore Installations Engaged in Oil and Gas Operations on the UK Continental Shelf[42] and MGN 704 (M+F) Prevention of Pollution: Prohibition on the Use, and Carriage for Use, of Heavy Fuel Oil in Arctic Waters[43] following amendments made under Merchant Shipping (Prevention of Oil Pollution) (Amendment) Regulations 2024 (SI 2024/1296).

Merchant Shipping (Prevention of Pollution by Sewage from Ships) Regulations 2020 ('Sewage Regulations')

Annex IV to MARPOL, as amended by the Protocol of 1978 are implemented by the Sewage Regulations. These Regulations apply to ships on international voyages, for UK ships wherever they may be including those operating in Polar waters and for other ships only if they are within UK waters. The requirements apply to ships of 400 gross tonnage or above and ships under 400 gross tonnage if they carry

42 *See:* https://www.gov.uk/government/publications/mgn-603m-requirements-for-oil-or-oily-mixture-discharges-for-offshore-installations-engaged-in-oil-and-gas-operations-on-the-uk-continental-shelf.

43 *See*: https://www.gov.uk/government/publications/mgn-704-mf-prevention-of-oil-pollution-prohibition-on-the-use-and-carriage-for-use-of-heavy-fuel-oil-in-arctic-waters/mgn-704-mf-prevention-of-oil-pollution-prohibition-on-the-use-and-carriage-for-use-of-heavy-fuel-oil-hfo-in-arctic-waters.

more than 15 persons[44]. There is a restriction on the jurisdiction of these offences when outside of the UK limits[45].

In essence, ships are prohibited from discharging sewage from a ship into the sea subject to some exceptions[46]. Sewage is defined in regulation 1, Annex IV to MARPOL as follows:

> '*3.1 drainage and other wastes from any form of toilets and urinals;*
>
> *3.2 drainage from medical premises (dispensary, sick bay, etc.) via wash basins, wash tubs and scuppers located in such premises;*
>
> *3.3 drainage from spaces containing living animals; or drainage from spaces containing living animals; or*
>
> *3.4 other waste waters when mixed with the drainages defined above.*'

Discharge is defined as: 'in *relation to sewage, means any release howsoever caused from a ship, and includes any escape, disposal, spilling, leaking, pumping, emitting or emptying*'. However, it is important to note that the prohibition under regulation 7 does not apply in the following circumstances:

a. If the discharge was necessary to secure the safety of the ship and those on board or to save a life at sea;

---

44 Regulation 6, Merchant Shipping (Prevention of Pollution by Sewage from Ships) Regulations 2020.

45 *See above,* regulation 33.

46 *See above,* regulation 7.

b. If it results from damage to the ship or equipment and all reasonable precautions were taken to prevent or minimise the discharge; or

c. The discharge took place in the jurisdiction of non-UK waters where requirements of that State may be less stringent.

Under regulations 8 and 9, a ship is expected to have appropriate equipment for the purposes of sewage as set out in MARPOL. A further requirement on UK ships proceeding to sea is that under regulation 11 they must not do so without a valid sewage certificate. There are similar prohibitions on non-UK ships under regulation 12.

Regulation 20 sets out responsibilities on owners and masters of UK ships ensuring that the condition of the ship and equipment conforms with the requirement to have a sewage system under part 3 of the Sewage Regulations to ensure that it is fit to proceed to sea without an unreasonable threat or harm to the marine environment. Owners and masters of UK ships are also responsible for reporting at the earliest opportunity, to the MCA[47] or to the maritime authority of the State which they are in, if defects are discovered or when an accident occurs if this substantially affects the integrity of the ship or efficiency or completeness of the equipment of the ship[48]. If corrective action advised by a surveyor is not taken within a specified time, by an owner and master of a vessel, the Sewage Certificate can be suspended[49].

Under regulation 25, inspectors have powers to inspect ships and to validate compliance with the Sewage Regulations. In essence those powers can only be exercised in UK waters or controlled waters. The

---

47 i.e. the Certifying Authority who issued the Sewage Certificate.

48 *See above,* regulation 20(3) & (4).

49 *See* above, regulation 22.

powers extend to the detention of a deficient ship if there are clear grounds for believing that if a vessel proceeds to sea, it will present an unreasonable threat of harm to the marine environment[50].

Contraventions of the Sewage Regulations are deemed to be a criminal offence by the owner and master under regulation 30. These include but are not limited to proceeding to sea without a Sewage Certificate (regulations 11 and 12(1), (2) or (3)), failing to comply with the master and owner's responsibilities of a UK ship (regulation 20(1), (2) or (3)), discharging sewage when prohibited to do so (regulation 7)[51] and not having the correct equipment and discharge connections as required under Annex IV (regulations 8 and 9).

The sentence for conviction on summary and indictment is a fine. For offences which do not comply with regulation 7, the financial penalty in the magistrates' court is limited to £250,000[52].

MGN 631 (M+F) Amendment 1[53] provides further guidance and clarification on the applicability of the MARPOL Annex IV, the Polar Code and Sewage Regulations and the Merchant Shipping (Prevention of Oil Pollution and Prevention of Pollution by Sewage from Ships) (Amendment) Regulations 2022.

---

50 *See above,* regulations 26 and 27.

51 In respect of a fixed or floating platform, this can be an offence by an owner and manager and the case of a ship other than a fixed or floating platform, this offence can be committed by the owner, manager, demise charterer and master of the ship.

52 *See* s.131(3) of MSA.

53 *See:* https://www.gov.uk/government/publications/mgn-631-mf-amendment-1-the-merchant-shipping-prevention-of-pollution-by-sewage-from-ships-regulations-2020.

It is important to be aware that these regulations have ambulatory effect meaning that if the Convention or Polar Code are modified or replaced, these are automatically applicable to the said Regulations without the implementation of any further UK law.

Merchant Shipping (Prevention of Pollution by Garbage from Ships) Regulations 2020 ('Garbage Regulations'):

These Regulations implement Annex V to MARPOL, as amended by the Protocol of 1978. Annex V contains regulations for the Prevention of Pollution by Garbage from Ship Under regulation 5 of the Garbage Regulations there is a prohibition on the discharge of garbage into the sea subject to a number of exceptions. They apply to UK ships wherever they may be and other ships that are within UK waters or controlled waters[54]. A UK ship must not enter the Antarctic area unless they have sufficient capacity for the retention of garbage on board[55].

Under regulation 10, it imposes a requirement for the carrying on ships, which have an overall length of 12 metres or more or is fixed or a floating platform, of placards notifying passengers and crew about the disposal of garbage. Ships which are 100GT or above, carry 15 people or more or are a fixed or a floating platform are required to have a garbage management plan as per regulation 11 and garbage record books to record the discharge, accidental loss or completed

54 'Controlled waters' means the areas of sea specified by the Merchant Shipping (Prevention of Pollution) (Limits) Regulations 2014 as waters within which the jurisdiction and rights of the United Kingdom are exercisable in accordance with Part XII of UNCLOS (Protection and Preservation of the Marine Environment).

55 Regulation 7 of Garbage Regulations.

incineration of garbage[56]. Ships without garbage record books are required to record certain discharges of garbage in their log-books.[57]

Contravention of the regulations are offences as set out in regulation 21 by owners and managers of the fixed or floating platforms and in the case of a ship, depending on the offence, by the owner, manager, demise charterer or the master of the ship. Specific restrictions are placed on the jurisdiction of offences outside the UK under regulation 23.

In England and Wales, the sentence for such offences are both punishable on summary and indictment conviction by a fine. MGN 632 (M + F) Amendment 2 provides further guidance on the Garbage Regulations alongside MARPOL Annex V and the International Code for Ships Operating in Polar Waters ('the Polar Code')[58].

Merchant Shipping (Prevention of Pollution from Noxious Liquid Substances in Bulk) Regulations 2018 ('NLS Regulations')

The NLS Regulations brought into force Annex II of MARPOL which applies largely to UK NLS ships or other NLS ships whilst in UK waters[59] also has ambulatory effect. The Regulations provides for

---

56 *See above,* regulations 12 and 13.

57 *See above,* regulation 15.

58 *See* https://www.gov.uk/government/publications/mgn-632-mf-amendment-2-the-merchant-shipping-prevention-of-pollution-by-garbage-from-ships-regulations-2020/mgn-632-mf-amendment-2-the-merchant-shipping-prevention-of-pollution-by-garbage-from-ships-regulations-2020.

59 Merchant Shipping (Prevention of Pollution from Noxious Liquid Substances in Bulk) Regulations 2018, regulation 5.

a survey and certification regime for ships engaged in the carriage of noxious liquid substances in bulk[60]. Regulation 13 sets out responsibilities on the owner and master of an NLS ship ensuring that the condition of the ship conforms with relevant requirements in order that it remains fit to proceed to sea without presenting an unreasonable threat of harm to the marine environment. An accident to the ship or a discovered defect which substantially affects its integrity, efficiency or completeness of the ship must be reported to the MCA at the earliest opportunity or to any other appropriate maritime certifying authority of the port where the accident or defect occurs.

The MCA will carry out an investigation to determine any necessary repairs or whether an additional survey is required. If a ship is deficient and it or its equipment does not correspond with the NLS certificate or the ship is unfit to proceed to sea without presenting an unreasonable threat of harm to the marine environment, the MCA can require corrective action to be taken[61].

It is prohibited under regulation 24 to discharge noxious liquid substance or ballast water, tank washings or other mixture containing a noxious liquid substance into the sea from any ship. There are exceptions to the prohibition such as if the discharge is necessary to secure the safety of the ship or for saving life or results from damage to the ship or its equipment and all reasonable precaution have been taken to prevent or minimise the discharge and the owner and master did not act intentionally or recklessly and with knowledge that damage would probably result. If a UK ship discharges noxious liquid substance and in doing so violates the regulations, this will become the

---

60 *See above,* regulation 9 and 13.

61 *See above,* regulation 20.

subject of an investigation[62]. In respect of on UK ships, there are restrictions on instituting proceedings if a prohibition offence is committed outside of the UK limits[63]. There is a further prohibition relating to the carriage and discharge of unassessed liquid substances, which have not been categorised under regulation 26. Further requirements on NLS ships include recording promptly in a Cargo Record Book at the completion of any operation[64], carrying on board an approved Procedure and Arrangements Manual[65] and for NLS ships which are 150 gross tonnage or more must carry on board a Marine Pollution Emergency Plan.[66]

As with other pollution regulations, the MCA has the power to inspect ships[67] to check compliance with the regulations and detain a ship[68] if there are clear grounds for doing so. Regulation 38 sets out which contraventions of the regulations amount to offences. The sentence for these offences is punishable by fine on summary conviction and conviction on indictment.

62 *See above,* regulation 33.

63 *See above,* regulation 41.

64 *See above,* regulation 29.

65 *See above,* regulation 28.

66 *See above,* regulation 30.

67 *See above,* regulation 33.

68 *See above,* regulation 34.

Merchant Shipping (Oil Pollution Preparedness, Response and Co-operation Convention) Regulations 1998:

Under regulation 4 there is a requirement on harbour authorities or an operator of an oil facility to have, submit, re-submit and maintain an oil pollution emergency plan. Failure to implement, submit or re-submit or maintain such a plan is an offence under regulation 7. A master of a UK ship whether that ship is in the UK, controlled water or when it is elsewhere has a duty to report to HM Coastguard or to the nearest coastal state if they become aware of any event or observe the discharge of oil at sea from another ship or from an offshore installation. A similar obligation attaches to a responsible person, an operator of an oil handling facility[69] and a harbour master or other individual having charge of a harbour and any individual in charge of an oil facility[70].

A contravention of regulation 4 is an offence punishable by fine both on summary conviction and conviction on indictment. The failure to report requirement under regulations 5 or 6 is also punishable by fine on conviction. This is unlimited on indictment but shall not exceed £5,000 on summary conviction[71].

69 Merchant Shipping (Oil Pollution Preparedness, Response and Co-operation Convention) Regulations 1998, regulation 5.

70 *See above,* regulation 6.

71 *See above,* regulation 7.

Breaches of Collision Regulations

The Merchant Shipping (Distress Signals and Prevention of Collisions) Regulations 1996

The International COLREGs[72] provide a number of rules and standards for vessels to abide by when navigating waters or the sea for the avoidance of a collision. However, their purpose is not only to avoid a collision but also the effects of a collision, if one were to occur. No definition of collision is given within the COLREGs or the The Merchant Shipping (Distress Signals and Prevention of Collisions) Regulations 1996 ('1996 Regulations'). However in case law, collision has been defined as damage sustained by a ship as a result of another ship coming into contact with her.[73]

Under regulation 4 of the 1996 Regulations all vessels are required to comply with the provisions of rules 1 to 36 of the International COLREGs. Any contravention of the Regulations is a criminal offence, which can be committed by the owner of the vessel, the master and any person who at the time was responsible for the conduct of the vessel. The 1996 Regulations must be read in conjunction with the International COLREGs or MSN 1781 (M+F) Amendment 3[74]. Therefore, for any prosecution to be brought under the 1996 Regulations, MSN 1781 (M + F) Amendment 3 and/or the International COLREGs will need to be reviewed very carefully to

---

72 *See*: https://treaties.un.org/doc/Publication/UNTS/Volume%201050/volume-1050-I-15824-English.pdf.

73 *See Everard v Kendall* (1870) LR 5 CP 428, 39 LJCP 234, 3 Mar LC 391, 18 WR 892, 22 LT 408; *The Normandy* [1904] P 187, 9 Asp MLC 568, DC; *The Upcerne* [1912] P 160, 12 Asp MLC 281.

74 *See:* https://www.gov.uk/government/publications/msn-1781-mf-amendment-3-the-merchant-shipping-regulations-1996-colreg.

determine if they apply to a vessel, which rule has been breached and whether any of the exemptions apply.

The 1996 Regulations not only applies to UK ships or ships within the UK's territory but also to sea planes and includes the definition of 'hovercraft' within the definition of a ship[75]. Since the Merchant Shipping (Watercraft) Order 2023, the regulations also apply to watercrafts[76].

The COLREGs contain 41 rules and are divided into 6 parts. These relate to the following topics:

- Part A: General;
- Part B: Steering and Sailing;
- Part C: Lights and Shapes;
- Part D: Sounds and Light Signals;
- Part E: Exemptions; and
- Part F: Verification of compliance with provisions of the Conventions

There are also 4 annexes which contain technical detail on lights and shapes and their positioning, sound signaling appliance, additional

---

75 *See* regulation 2 of The Merchant Shipping (Distress Signals and Prevention of Collisions) Regulations 1996.

76 *See* schedule 2, Merchant Shipping (Watercraft) Order 2023.

signals for finishing vessels when operating in close proximity and international distress signals.

In collision cases, the MCA largely prosecutes under the 1996 Regulations and s.58 of the Merchant Shipping Act 1995 which is referred to below. In general terms, contraventions of the 1996 Regulations are punishable on conviction by a term of imprisonment not exceeding 2 years and a fine or on summary conviction by a fine[77].

Unsafe Operations

The Merchant Shipping (International Safety Management (ISM) Code) Regulations 2014

Under s.85 of the MSA, the Secretary of State can make regulations for the safety and health on ships. One such regulation which implements the International Safety Management Code ('ISM Code') is the Merchant Shipping (International Safety Management (ISM) Code) Regulations 2014 ('ISM Code Regulations 2014'). The purpose of the ISM Code is to ensure safety of life at sea, prevent human injury and loss of life, avoid damage to the environment (particularly the marine environment) and avoid damage to property. The ISM Code came about due to the significant concern about poor management standards in shipping. The ISM Code Regulations 2014 implements Regulation (EC) 336/2006 of the European Parliament which made the IMO's ISM Code directly applicable in EU member states. In essence the ISM Code Regulations 2014 requires companies

[77] *See* The Merchant Shipping (Distress Signals and Prevention of Collisions) Regulations 1996, regulation 6.

to implement Safety Management Systems ('SMS')[78] for their ships and encourages a safety culture within the shipping industry.

As highlighted in a previous chapter an ISM Company is either the owner of a ship or is a person who is not the owner of the ship but who has taken over the duties and responsibilities under the ISM for the operation of the ship.[79] The ISM Code Regulations 2014 set out a number of requirements on an ISM Company including holding:

a. a valid Document of Compliance ('DOC')[80] or Interim Compliance in respect of a ship which must be carried on board of the ship;

b. a valid Safety Management Certificate ('SMC') or Interim Safety Management certificate which has been issued and the original must be carried on board[81].

---

78 Under 1.1.4 of the ISM Code an SMS means a structured and documented system enabling company personnel to implement effectively the Company safety and environmental policy.

79 *See* ISM Code Regulations, reg 2.

80 When the shore side aspects of the safety management system complies with the ISM Code, a DOC will be issued to a Company.

81 *See* above, reg 6.

A DOC is a document that is issued to an ISM Company when it complies with the requirement of the ISM Code (1.1.5 of the ISM Code). An SMC means a document issued to a ship which signifies that the Company and its shipboard management operate in accordance with the approved SMS (1.1.6 of the ISM Code). These documents are deemed invalid if they have not been adequately audited[82]. As the MCA have direct responsibility for the assessment and audit of UK Shipping companies and ships against the ISM Code, they have the power to issue the DOCs and SMCs. These are not valid for more than 5 years.

The MCA also has the power to suspend or cancel a DOC or SMC if there is a major non-conformity with the ISM Code.

Under regulation 7 of the ISM Regulations 2014, the master of a ship must operate a ship in accordance with the SMS as per the SMC. Under regulation 8 an ISM Company must designate someone to maintain and implement the SMS and ensure compliance with it, monitor the safe and efficient operation of the that ship and to ensure that the ship is properly manned, equipped and maintained so it operates in accordance with the SMS.

---

82 *See* above, reg 6(2)(c).

It is an offence to contravene provisions which require compliance with the ISM Code as set out at regulation 15 of the ISM Code Regulations 2014 punishable by a fine, on summary conviction not exceeding the statutory maximum against the ISM Company or on indictment by a fine. An offence against the Master or Designated person is punishable on summary conviction by a fine, not exceeding the statutory maximum or on conviction on indictment by imprisonment not exceeding two years or a fine or both.

The MCA has provided statutory guidance[83] for surveyors auditing SMS at sea and ashore and it is a useful tool to understand how the ISM procedures are to be adopted.

The MCA have recently concluded a consultation on a proposal to make the Merchant Shipping (International Safety Management (ISM) Code) Regulations 2025. These new regulations intend to consolidate existing legislation including the UK assimilated version of Regulation (EC) 336/2006 on the implementation of the International ISM Code and the ISM Code Regulations 2014 into one set of regulations that will require compliance with the International ISM Code. The latest proposal seeks to apply to any shipping service and not just 'regular shipping service' and it will also apply to Ro-Ro[84] passenger ferries and high-speed craft operating in the UK.

83 *See* https://www.gov.uk/government/publications/the-ism-code-msis-2/msis-2-international-management-code-for-the-safe-operation-of-ships-and-for-pollution-prevention-the-ism-code--2#part-b--certification-and-verification.

84 Ro-Ro ferries refers to roll on-roll off ferries where vehicles such as cars, buses, motorcycles, etc can drive on and off.

Merchant Shipping (Vessels in Commercial Use for Sport of Pleasure) Regulations 2025

Another such regulation which focuses on vessel safety is the Merchant Shipping (Vessels in Commercial Use for Sport of Pleasure) Regulations 2025 which gives legal effect to The Safety of Small Vessels in Commercial Use for Sport or Pleasure – A Code of Practice ('Sport or Pleasure Vessel Code')[85]. The new Code was introduced on 12 December 2025 and was brought in to replace and consolidate the old Yellow Blue, Red and Intended Pleasure Vessel Codes[86], and Marine Guidance Note 280, which together was cumbersome and, at times, difficult to enforce. The Sport or Pleasure Vessel Code however provides one single framework to ensure safety and compliance requirements at sea for small vessels under 24 metres which are used commercially for sport or pleasure, carry no cargo and a maximum of 12 passengers. It has also been modernised to reflect changing technology, safety practices and environmental considerations.

It is important to be aware that the Sport or Pleasure Vessel Code does not apply to vessels that operate underwater, hovercrafts or vessels which carry cargo. The activities covered by the code include vessels engaged in racing, high speed crafts carrying passengers on sightseeing trips and vessel operating as beachcraft which are in commercial use.

---

85 *See* https://assets.publishing.service.gov.uk/media/691e23cb513046b952c500df/The_sport_or_pleasure_vessel_code.pdf

86 The replaced codes are as follows: The Safety of Small Commercial Motor Vessels" (1998) (The Yellow Code), The Safety of Small Commercial Sailing Vessels (1998) (The Blue Code), The Safety of Small Vessels in Commercial Use for Sport or Pleasure Operating from a Nominated Departure Point (2000) (The Red Code) and The Code of Practice for Intended Pleasure Vessels in Temporary Commercial Use at Sea (2019) (The IPV Code).

The Merchant Shipping (Vessels in Commercial Use for Sport of Pleasure) Regulations 2025 also gives effect to the existing Red Ensign Group Yacht Code ('REG Yacht Code') setting out safety compliance and pollution prevention for yachts which are over 24 metres[87].

Safety requirements under the regulations include a requirement for large vessels to be subject to surveys and be issued with a valid certificate of compliance and further certification under the REG Yacht Code before they can proceed, attempt to proceed to sea or any voyage[88]. Similar obligations apply to small vessel which must not proceed or attempt to proceed to sea or on any voyage unless it has been subject to a survey or has been issued with a valid Small Sport or Pleasure Code Certificate[89]. Subject to the regulations on validity of certificates[90], cancellation of certificates[91] and deficient vessels[92], certification for large and small vessels are valid for no more than 5 years[93].

Further responsibilities are placed on owners and masters of vessels certified under these provisions to ensure that vessels and their equipment are maintained so they are fit to go to sea without danger and following a survey of the vessel no changes are made to the vessel

---

87 REG Yacht Code, Part A applies to Large Yacht Code up to 12 passengers and Part B applies to Passenger Yacht Code up to 36 passengers.

88 The Merchant Shipping (Vessels in Commercial Use for Sport of Pleasure) Regulations 2025, regulation 8.

89 *See* above, regulation 12.

90 *See* above, regulation 16.

91 *See* above, regulation 17.

92 *See* above, regulation 22.

93 *See* above, regulation 14.

by way of structural arrangements, machinery, equipment and any other item under the survey without prior authority from the Certifying Authority, i.e. the MCA[94].

It is also noteworthy that the new Regulations specify a reporting requirement on masters and owners for certified small and large vessels which may be involved in an 'incident' such as a collision, a grounding, a fire, or any other event connected to the operation of a vessel which has endangered or could endanger the safety of a vessel, its occupants or any other person or environment[95].

For any vessel which proceeds to or attempts to proceed to sea or on a voyage, non-compliance of the requirements under the Regulations is a criminal offence, for which both owner and master can be guilty[96]. Sentence for such offences are a fine on summary conviction[97] and conviction on indictment, a term of imprisonment not exceeding 2 years, a fine or both.

Merchant Shipping and Fishing Vessels (Health and Safety at Work) Regulations 1997

The Merchant Shipping and Fishing Vessels (Health and Safety at Work) Regulations 1997 sets out a framework of health and safety on board ships similar to the obligations laid down in Health and Safety at Work etc Act 1974 and the Management of Health and Safety at Work Regulations 1999. The 1997 Regulations implements aspects

---

94 *See* above, regulation 21(1).

95 *See* above, regulation 21(2) & (4).

96 *See* above, regulation 23.

97 These are limited to the statutory maximum in Northern Ireland and Scotland.

of the Maritime Labour Convention 2006 but also places duties on the ship owner and the employer and places a duty of care on all seafarers regardless of their employment status[98].

The regulations apply to work activities on United Kingdom ships anywhere in the world, and to non-UK ships when they are in United Kingdom water[99]. Part 2 of the Regulations sets out the general duties on the health and safety of the worker and includes matters like health and safety policy, risk assessment, night work and health surveillance. Part 3 details the duties of the Company and Part 4 sets out Special Responsibilities for Health and Safety and Consultation with Workers. A contravention of each separate duty is a criminal offence under regulation 24. Depending on the breach of the regulation, the sentence ranges from a fine to a term of imprisonment not exceeding two years.

Code of Safe Working Practices for Merchant Seafarers

The Code of Safe Working Practices for Merchant Seafarers[100] provides best practice on health and safety on board a ship from issues such as living on board to manual handling and hot works. Statutory duties are explained in the Code and practical advice is given for safe working on board. The Code largely reflects the obligations for standards of safety, equipment or operations. Therefore, the Code has

---

98 *See* Merchant Shipping and Fishing Vessels (Health and Safety at Work) Regulations 1997, regulations 4, 5, 13, 13A and 21.

99 *See above,* regulation 3.

100 *See* Code of Safe Working Practices for Seafarers 2025 edition: https://assets.publishing.service.gov.uk/media/67e527b5a82c168e578c9b5a/12464_MCA_COSWP_BLACK_AND_WHITE_v3_0W.pdf.

no statutory status and does not supersede the regulations. However, compliance with it indicates to the MCA that a company or employer have done what was reasonable to comply with the regulations, which can be play a key role when defending offences brought under the Merchant Shipping and Fishing Vessels (Health and Safety at Work) Regulations 1997.

In the Merchant Shipping (Code of Safe Working Practices) (amendments and revocation) regulations 2015 there is a duty on the shipowner to ensure that the code of safe working practices for merchant seafarers is easily accessible and readily available to all those working on board their ships.

Ship dangerously unsafe

A master and/or owner of a vessel are guilty of an offence if their ship is deemed dangerously unsafe under s.98 of MSA, if their ship is in a port in the UK. This section does however recognise that with many ships, responsibilities relating to safety can be delegated to other persons through the terms of a charterparty or management agreement and therefore if such responsibility has been assumed by others at time that a ship is dangerously unsafe, then the person(s) other than the owner may be guilty of an offence. The terms of the charterparty will need to be carefully reviewed to understand the extent of the duties of any third party for health and safety compliance onboard a ship.

If a vessel is 'dangerously unsafe' and therefore unfit to go on a voyage or remain at sea without there being a serious danger to human life, the MCA are likely to engage their power to detain that ship[101]. Reasons for an unsafe ship can include amongst other things a defective hull and/or machinery, undermanning, overloading or

---

[101] *See* s.94 and 95 of above.

unsafe or improper loading or any other matter affecting the safety of the ship. The question of whether a ship is dangerously unsafe will be a question of law and fact, which is likely to be supported by expert evidence.

For such an offence a sentence of a financial penalty is attributable in both a conviction on summary and indictment. However, in a conviction on indictment, the Court's sentencing powers can also include a term of imprisonment of up to two years.

Conduct endangering masters and crew

The most serious of the MCA's prosecutions fall under s.58 of the MSA. Under s.58 there is a general duty relating to all seamen employed on a UK ship including the master to avoid endangering the ship, any other ship, structure[102] or any other person. The duty extends to seamen on a UK registered ship and any ship registered to another country which is in a UK port or within UK waters[103].

The duty arises for an individual if their act or omission was:

a. deliberate; or

b. amounted to a breach or neglect[104] of duty; or

---

[102] *See* MSA 1995, s.58(8)(b): 'structure' is defined as any fixed or movable structure other than a ship.

[103] *See above,* s.58(1).

[104] *See above,* s.58(8): 'except in relation to a master, includes any disobedience to a lawful command'

c. if the master or seaman was under the influence of drink or drug at the time of the act or omission[105].

An offence is committed if the act causes or is likely to cause the loss or destruction of or serious damage to a ship, its machinery, navigational equipment or safety equipment, to any other ship or any structure or death of or serious injury to any person. Similarly it is also an offence if a master or seaman omits to do anything required to preserve his ship, its machinery, navigational equipment or safety equipment from being lost, destroyed or seriously damaged, or omits to preserve from death or serious injury any person either on board his ship or not on board his ship, or prevents his ship from causing loss of destruction or serious damage to any other ship or structure[106].

In *Goodwin* the Court of Appeal quashed Mr Goodwin's conviction and sentence under s.58 of MSA for which he was prosecuted following an incident in which his jet ski collided with a stationary jet ski causing serious injury to the other rider. For the purposes of the MSA, a jet ski was not defined as a ship and therefore Mr Goodwin could not be prosecuted under s.58 as it was deemed not to be 'used in navigation'[107]. However, following the Watercraft Order 2023, s.58 is now applicable to watercrafts such as jet skis alongside ships and fishing vessels, as it is intended under the MSA. At this time, however,

---

105 *See above,* s.58(3).

106 *See above,* s.58(2)(b).

107 In *Goodwin,* Lord Phillips CJ stated at para 33: *"We have concluded that those authorities which confine "vessel used in navigation" to vessels which are used to make ordered progression over the water from one place to another are correctly decided. The words "used in navigation" exclude from the definition of "ship or vessel" craft that are simply used for having fun on the water without the object of going anywhere, into which category jet skis plainly fall."*

it is understood that non-power-driven and unmanned crafts still fall outside of the criminal regime of s.58 and the COLREGs[108]. Therefore, the nature of the vessel will need to be carefully considered before a prosecution can be brought under s.58 of the MCA or any of the other safety related offences.

The sentence for a person convicted of an offence under s.58 of MCA, is a term of imprisonment not exceeding 2 years or fine or both for a conviction on indictment and a fine for a person on summary conviction.

At the time of writing this book, the MCA has successfully prosecuted Adam Russell in its first ever prosecution under the Watercraft Order 2023 following the collision of Mr Russell's speedboat with a fifteen-year-old kayaker near Milford Haven. Mr Russell was convicted in December 2025 of two offences: firstly failing without reasonable excuse to prevent the loss or destruction of another watercraft and/or serious injury to another person, contrary to Section 6 of the Merchant Shipping (Watercraft) Order 2023 and secondly failing without reasonable excuse to comply with the International COLREGS, namely failing to adhere to keeping a proper look out (rule 5), proceeding at a safe speed (rule 6) and risk of collision (rule 7), contrary to Section 6 of The Merchant Shipping (Distress Signals and Prevention of Collisions) Regulations 1996. He received a suspended prison sentence alongside a 15-hour activity requirement, 200 hours unpaid work, compensation and costs.

---

[108] The Application of the Merchant Shipping (Watercraft) Order 2023 JIML 29 (2023) 4, 237–241, 1 August 2023, Dan Smith, Master Mariner, University of Portsmouth.

Alcohol and Drug Offences

As an alternative to a prosecution under s.58 MSA, the MCA can bring proceedings against a professional pilot, seaman or master of a ship whose ability to carry out their duty is impaired by reason of drink or drugs is under s.78 of the Railway and Transport Act 2003 ('RTA 2003'). The pilot, seaman or master is only a professional if they act in the course of a business or employment[109]. Non-professionals on board a ship underway and who exercise a function in connection with the navigation of the ship, can also be prosecuted for undertaking that task if impaired by drink or drug[110]. The prescribed limits of alcohol in blood, breath and urine are set out in s.81 of RTA 2003, which has been updated by Merchant Shipping (Alcohol) (Prescribed Limits Amendment) Regulations 2015. Under these provisions statutory alcohol limits are in place for mariners and there is an alcohol and drug testing regime under s.83 of RTA 2003.

However, there is still no similar offence for non-professional mariners who are navigating a ship when under the influence of alcohol or drugs. Sections 80(1) to (3) of RTA 2003 have not yet come into force despite being provisions within the statute for over 20 years. The ongoing campaign for a change to this loophole within the law continues from those within the maritime industry such as from the British Ports Association.[111] This lack of legislation prohibiting the use of alcohol and drugs by those at the helm of a private or pleasure vessel has also been of concern to Coroners as noted in the prevention of future death report issued following the sad death of David Haw in

---

109 *See* Railways and Transport Act 2003, s.78(4).

110 *See above,* s.80.

111 *See* https://www.britishports.org.uk/government-must-close-drink-and-boat-loophole-when-toughening-drink-drive-laws/.

May 2022[112]. Whilst there is no legislative prohibition, for non-professional seaman, the Court treat being impaired by drink and drugs as an aggravating feature of a s.58 offence or under the 1996 Regulations[113].

Carriage of dangerous goods

Over the years there have been a number of prosecutions by the MCA for the dangerous carriage of goods. Prosecutions have been historically brought under the Merchant Shipping (Dangerous Goods and Marine Pollutants) Regulations 1997 for the transportation of dangerous goods. However, the Merchant Shipping (Carriage of Dangerous Goods and Harmful Substances) (Amendment) Regulations 2024 which came into force in June 2024 has amended and substantially replaced and/or revoked the following regulations:

- The Merchant Shipping (Dangerous Goods and Marine Pollutants) Regulations 1997;
- The Merchant Shipping (Gas Carriers) Regulations 1994; and

---

112 See https://www.judiciary.uk/prevention-of-future-death-reports/david-haw-prevention-of-future-deaths-report/.

113 *See* the conviction of Ian Sullivan who when under the influence grounded his vessel 'Sully' in Totland Bay, Isle of Wight for failure to keep a proper lookout and failure to proceed at a safe speed under The Merchant Shipping (Distress Signals and Prevention of Collisions) Regulations 1996 at https://www.gov.uk/government/news/boat-owner-to-pay-20000-after-vessel-collides-with-rocks.

- the Merchant Shipping (Carriage of Packaged Irradiated Nuclear Fuel etc) (INF Code) Regulations 2000.

The purpose of the new 2024 Regulations is to update and consolidate the legal framework on the carriage of dangerous goods and harmful substances by sea. To this end, specific requirements are set out for the transportation of different forms of dangerous goods and harmful substances. These have been divided into the following parts:

a. Part 2: requirements for carrying dangerous goods and harmful substances in package form;

b. Part 3: requirements for carrying dangerous goods and harmful substances in solid form in bulk;

c. Part 4: requirements for the construction and equipment of ships carrying dangerous liquid chemicals in bulk;

d. Part 5: requirements for the construction and equipment of ships carrying liquified chemicals in bulk;

e. Part 6: requirements for the carriage of packaged irradiated nuclear fuel, plutonium and high-level radioactive wastes on board ships.

Under Part 7 and specifically regulation 28 there are mandatory reporting requirements on the master and owner of the ship to report incidents involving dangerous goods in packaged form, in solid form in bulk and those involving harmful substances. The reporting requirements also extends to circumstances where pollution is likely to result from the discharge or threat of discharge from the cargo of a ship into UK waters or the UK coastline[114]. Non-compliance with the requirements under the regulations are a criminal offence which can be brought against the owner and master under regulation 31 or shipper[115] and forwarder[116] under regulation 32.

For all ships of 300 gross tonnage and above and fishing vessels, traditional ships, and recreational craft with a length of 45 metres and above there is a requirement under Merchant Shipping (Vessel Traffic Monitoring and Reporting Requirements) Regulations 2004 (as amended) to notify the port authority at least 24 hours in advance of entry into a UK port[117]. All ships, regardless of their size, are also required to report to the MCA before they depart from or if they are bound to a UK port if they are carrying dangerous goods or polluting goods[118]. Annex B of MSN 1899 sets out the information to be notified in accordance with regulation 10.

---

114 *See* regulation 29 of Merchant Shipping (Carriage of Dangerous Goods and Harmful Substances) (Amendment) Regulations 2024

115 Under regulation 3, a shipper is *'a person who, whether as principal or agent for another, consigns for carriage by sea dangerous goods or harmful substances'*

116 Under regulation 3, a forwarder is defined as *'the person by whom the dangerous goods declaration or marine pollutants declaration and packing certificate are received, and any person responsible for packing the goods into a cargo transport unit, for eventual delivery to the ship or its agent'*

117 Merchant Shipping (Vessel Traffic Monitoring and Reporting Requirements) Regulations 2004, regulation 5.

118 *See above,* regulation 10.

Failure to comply with regulation 10 is an offence by the owner, agent and master of the ship which is punishable by a fine on summary conviction and conviction by indictment[119].

Fraudulent completion of seafarer documentation

A real and growing problem within the maritime industry is the fraudulent completion of seafarer documentation. This can include the completion of certificates, information for purposes of completing a survey, entry of false records in registers.

Within various regulations, there are offences which relate to the creation or alteration of false documents. Within most of the pollution regulations, there is a corresponding prohibition which criminalises a person for intentionally altering, intentionally making, knowingly or recklessly providing false information certificates and surveys[120]. Further examples include s.14 of MSA, which states that it is an offence to make a statement which is known to be false or is made false recklessly in respect of any manner that is relevant to the British connection of a ship.

However, one of the most prolific concerns for the shipping industry, which can lead to dangerous consequences on board a ship have been fraudulent certificates of competency of Standards of Training, Certification and Watchkeeping for Seafarers ('STCW'). There can also be circumstances where authentic certificates are issued based on forged foreign documents. The Merchant Shipping (Standards of

[119] *See above,* regulation 17.

[120] Merchant Shipping (Prevention of Pollution from Noxious Liquid Substances in Bulk) Regulations, regulation 23; The Merchant Shipping (Prevention of Pollution by Sewage from Ships) Regulations 2020, regulation 24;

Training, Certification and Watchkeeping) Regulations 2022 specifies mandatory standards of competence, and training and certification requirements for seafarers on board merchant ships and make detailed provision to ensure the safe manning of ships in UK waters. The Merchant Shipping (Boatmasters' Qualifications, Crew and Hours of Work) Regulations 2015 sets out the requirements of crew competence and certification for the masters of all passenger and non-passenger vessels operating in the UK.

Under s.47(5) of MSA, it is an offence if a person makes a statement which he knows to be false or recklessly makes a statement which is false to obtain for himself or another a certificate or other document. This is punishable by way of a fine.

To tackle shipping fraud and enhance safety and security in shipping, the Merchant Shipping (Special Measures to Enhance Maritime Safety) Regulations 2024 was implemented. These regulations apply to most types of ships. In essence they require a vessel to have a ship identification number and keep a continuous synopsis record which is a complete history of the operations on a ship.

Other maritime offences prosecuted by different authorities

Pilotage Act 1987 ('PA 1987')

Misconduct by a pilot for endangering ships or persons on board is set out at s.21 of PA 1967. The duties of a pilot largely correspond to those set out under s.58 of MSA.

Guidance is provided by the MCA on management of ports and other marine facilities including the duties relating to pilotage activity. This guidance is called 'A guide to good practice on port and marine facilities'[121] and it should be read alongside the Code.

It is important to be aware that Competent Harbour Authorities ('CHA') have control over pilotage services under PA 1967 therefore they enforce responsibility under the Act including all prosecutions.

Corporate Manslaughter and Corporate Homicide Act 2007 ('CMCHA 2007')

Two maritime accidents and subsequent failed prosecutions following the 1987 Herald of Free Enterprise disaster and Marchioness disaster, paved the way for CMCHA 2007. If an organisation causes the death of an individual from the manner in which his activities are managed or organised and there has been a gross breach of relevant duty to the deceased owed by that organisation, then they can be prosecuted for corporate manslaughter under s.1 of the CMCHA 2007.

Such an offence applies to corporations, department or other body, police force or partnership, trade union or employer's association that is an employer.

As set out above the police are the lead prosecutor for such offences but they can be supported in their investigation by the MCA and HSE.

[121] *See* https://www.gov.uk/government/publications/a-guide-to-good-practice-on-port-marine-operations/a-guide-to-good-practice-on-port-and-marine-facilities.

Time Limits to prosecute

As with other criminal offences, the MSA has placed time limits on when offences must be prosecuted by.

Summary only offences which are to be prosecuted under the MSA are subject to a time limit as set out at s.274. If proceedings are not commenced within 6 months from the date that the offence was committed, a person cannot be convicted of a summary only offence. If during that period of 6 months, the accused leaves the United Kingdom, then proceedings must commence within 2 months after that person arrives within the United Kingdon and within 3 years of the date on which the offence was first committed.

The same limitations do not apply to indictable only offences.

However, there are exceptions to the time limit rule. The MCA can bring a prosecution within 3 years of the date when the offence was committed *if* the prosecution is brought within 6 months of the date that the MCA consider they have sufficient evidence to justify that prosecution of the offence came to their knowledge.

Defences to Prosecution

Most of the legislation for which the MCA can prosecute will have a defence for the corporation or individual in order that they can avoid liability. There are quite a few offences which are strict liability offences and do not require a *mens rea* or intention. However the main thrust of the defences within the maritime legislation relate to the reasonableness of the actions taken. Therefore with most offences it will be for the accused to prove on the *balance of probabilities* that they took all reasonable precautions and/or exercised due diligence to avoid committing an offence. This is known as the 'due diligence' offence, which many practitioners will be familiar with.

With certain offences there may be a third-party defence in addition to the due diligence offence where a company may have management agreement or charter party agreement with responsibility for a ship's safety has been delegated to others[122]. Unusually in the Prevention of Oil Pollution Regulations, alongside the defence of all reasonable steps, a further defence includes proving the ship was not a UK ship, the discharge took place in non-UK waters and the ship was in a UK port by reason of stress of weather or any other reason beyond the control of the master, owner or any charterer or manager[123].

It will therefore be necessary to consider carefully the wording of the legislation specific to an offence that has been charged as the terminology that is used to defend an offence can be partly altered as per the elements of the said offence.

Other supporting documentation relied on by the MCA

The MCA have created and published a series of Marine notes and notices which help to better understand and interpret the applicable laws and regulations that apply to different types of vessels, their owners and crew.

These are as follows:

Marine Guidance Notes ('MGNs')[124]***:*** These provide greater clarity on the interpretation of laws, regulations and give advice on various

---

122 *See* for example s.98(5), MSA.

123 *See* Merchant Shipping (Prevention of Oil Pollution) Regulations 2019, regulation 47

124 *See* MGNs at https://www.gov.uk/government/collections/marine-guidance-notices-mgns.

maritime issues such as safety, training, inspections compliance and ship operations. Although the MGNs provide helpful guidance notes explaining the law and/or the requirements on various compliance issues, it is important to note that they are simply guidance and are not legally binding. The applicability of the MGNs can be a hotly contested issue within court proceedings. However, as of yet, no higher court has determined the status of an MGN.

Merchant Shipping Notices ('MSNs')[125]*:* These are notices that must be complied with as they explain technical details set out in the associated regulations. These are also helpful guides to further amplify the meaning of the requirements within a set of regulations or explain any amendments.

Marine Information Notes ('MINs')[126]*:* The MCA provides information in MINs which are valid for a specific and short period of time and tend to be relevant to small groups. Examples of MINs can relate to a variety of issues but these have previously included changes to written examinations, examination arrangements, updates on maritime codes and protocols and amendments to a VHF channel.

MCA Safety Bulletins[127]*:* These bulletins are safety alerts relating to specific issues that identify a hazard or an issue arising from a near miss, accident or as a result of survey testing. These have included

125 *See* MSNs at https://www.gov.uk/government/collections/merchant-shipping-notices-msns

126 *See* MINs at https://www.gov.uk/government/collections/marine-information-notes-mins

127 *See* MCA Safety Bulletins at https://www.gov.uk/government/collections/maritime-and-coastguard-agency-mca-safety-bulletins

errors in marine equipment, updates on health and safety guidance and requirements on life saving equipment.

Within the title of both MSNs and MINs, it can be immediately identified which type of vessel they relate to, from the suffix used. So for merchant ships the suffix is an '(M)', '(F)' for fishing vessels or for both merchant ships and fishing vessels, it is '(M+F)'.

Sentence

The sentence for each offence is set out in the specific legislation. Unlike many other offences, there are no specific sentencing guidelines from the Sentencing Council which apply to breaches of maritime legislation. Therefore, for sentence, the Court will apply the general duty of a court on sentencing as set out in s.59 of the Sentencing Act 2020[128]. The Sentencing Council's 'General Guideline: Overarching Principles'[129] provides a helpful starting point and confirms that the Court should take account of the following factors if they apply:

a. the statutory maximum sentence (and if appropriate minimum sentence) for the offence;

b. sentencing judgments of the Court of Appeal (Criminal Division) for the offence; and

c. definitive sentencing guidelines for analogous offences.

---

128 *See* also *R v Sandhu* [2017] EWCA Crim 908, para 21

129 *See* https://sentencingcouncil.org.uk/guidelines/general-guideline-overarching-principles/?source=7511

In respect of offending behaviour which relates to unsafe operations or conduct endangering master and crew, the analogous sentencing guidelines tends to be the Sentencing Council's 'Health and Safety Offences, Corporate Manslaughter and Food Safety and Hygiene Offences' Definitive Guidelines. For pollution offences, the Court can be referred to the analogous sentencing guidelines from the Sentencing Council for 'Unauthorised or harmful deposit, treatment or disposal etc of waste and Illegal discharges to air, land and water' for either individuals or organisations. In the recent prosecution of Adam Russell, in which his speedboat crashed into a kayaker whilst travelling at an unsafe speed, the Court took the view that the 'Dangerous Driving' Sentencing Council Guidelines was most analogous to the incident he was dealing with. When passing sentence, the Judge stated: *'Just like our roads, our seas and our rivers are not playgrounds. They are required by all of us to recognise the risk to others innocently going about their business'*[130].

Generally, when considering what sentence to impose, the Court will follow the below stepped approach:

a. Step 1: the seriousness of an offence in the usual way by considering the culpability of the offender and the harm caused by the offending;

b. Step 2: considering whether there are any aggravating factors which make the offence more serious or any mitigating factors which may reduce the seriousness of the offence;

c. Step 3: whether there are factors which indicate a reduction for assistance to the prosecution;

130 See https://www.gov.uk/government/news/speedboat-driver-who-hit-teen-kayaker-first-to-be-sentenced-under-new-safety-law.

d. Step 4: whether there should be any reduction for a guilty plea[131];

e. Step 5: dangerousness (this issue is unlikely to apply to breaches of maritime law);

f. Step 6: special custodial sentence for certain offenders of particular concern;

g. Step 7: apply the totality principle considering whether the total sentence is just and proportionate to the overall offending behaviour;

h. Step 8: whether to make a compensation and/or ancillary orders:

i. Step 9: the Court must give reasons for sentence;

j. Step 10: the Court must consider if credit should be given for time spent on bail.

The above list may differ slightly when applying the analogous sentencing guidelines but they provide a helpful guide to follow when advising on the issue of sentence. The MCA provide prosecution lists for each year of their convictions which can be used to assist lawyers in understanding the types and levels of sentences handed down in specific cases. However it is important to note that these cases are fact specific and the detail provided in the prosecution lists can be quite limited unless further information regarding these cases can be established from the MCA.

---

131 *See* Sentencing Council Guidelines on 'Reduction in Sentence for a guilty plea – first hearing on or after 1 June 2017'

It is important to note that there are very few Judges in the criminal courts who will be familiar with the law and sentence relating to maritime offending. Therefore, a sentencing note from the prosecution and defence will provide considerable assistance to the Court at the time of sentence.

CHAPTER FOUR

FURTHER POWERS OF MCA

Alongside a criminal prosecution, the MCA have a number of administrative and/or ancillary sanctions or powers at their disposal. It is important to be aware of what these are as they are frequently used during the investigation process and post prosecution.

These main ancillary powers of the MCA are as follows:

Inspection and follow up

Under s. 258 of MSA 1995, MCA officers and surveyors have, in broad terms, been given powers to go onboard a ship in the United Kingdom or in UK waters and inspect the ship, its equipment any article onboard and any document carried within it, at all reasonable times, to ensure compliance with the rules and regulations of MSA 1995. This power extends to a UK ship outside of UK waters[132]. However, it does not apply to a foreign ship which is exercising its right of innocent passage or one that is transiting through straits which are used for international navigation[133].

---

132 *See* s.258(1) of MSA 1995.

133 *See* s.258(1A) of above.

Obstructing an officer exercising the power to inspect a vessel is a criminal offence in itself and is liable on summary conviction to a fine[134].

In most cases, the MCA will exercise this power in circumstances where there has been a collision, sinking, major mechanical failure or if there has been a fatality, serious injury or damage to a vessel.

A ship must not be unnecessarily detained or delayed if there is a necessity for the ship to be taken into dock for the hull or machinery to be surveyed[135].

The extent of an MCA inspector or officer's power to inspect a ship or premises is set out at s.259 of MSA 1995. This relates to any premises in the UK or any UK ship anywhere in the world or any other ship in the UK or in UK waters. S.259 allows an inspector to enter any premises or board any ship if it believes it is necessary for him to do so. In performing their functions, an inspector has the power as part of their investigation to take possession and detain equipment or materials to examine them, take photographs or measurements, require items not to be disturbed or cause an article to be dismantled or tested, take samples, request information and require the inspection or production of books or documents, amongst other things[136]. Some of these powers are similar to police powers of entry and seizure under Code B of the Police and Crime and Evidence Act 1984. However, although the MCA will need a good reason to inspect a ship or premises, it is not required to obtain a search warrant authorised by a Court.

---

134 *See* s.258(5) of above.

135 *See* s.258(3) of above.

136 *See* s.259(2) of above.

The purpose of these inspections is to ensure that a vessel is compliant with all the relevant standards and that at the time of an accident, working practices are adequate and conform with the rules.

Additionally, if an officer has reason to suspect that there may be noncompliance of the law by a merchant seaman, there is a power in which they can require the owner, master or any crew member to produce the ship's documents[137].

Improvement and Prohibition Notices

As with other enforcement agencies, the MCA has the power to issue improvement notices in which it can compel the responsible person to take steps to make an activity or vessel safe[138]. It may also serve a prohibition notice, stopping any further activity from taking place if there is a risk of serious personal injury to any person or serious pollution on navigable waters[139]. The risk of serious personal injury does not have to be on board a ship.

Such notices do not need to specify what action or measures needs to be taken to remedy the situation.

Any objections to reasonableness or valid basis for the improvement and/or prohibition notice must be made to the inspector within 21 days of service of the notice. The decision on any such dispute is to be made by a single arbitrator appointed by agreement of the parties. In

---

137 *See* s.257 of above.

138 *See* s.261 of above

139 *See* s.262 of above.

certain circumstances, compensation can be awarded by an arbitrator if a party successfully challenges the prohibition notice.

Breaches of an improvement notice or prohibition notice is a criminal offence under s.266 of MSA unless the Defendant can prove that they exercise all due diligence in breaching the notice. Such offences are liable to a fine on summary conviction or conviction on indictment.

Notification of Concern

In the event that the MCA has insufficient evidence to prosecute or issue a caution for a breach of the merchant shipping legislation but there is cause for concern, it may write a letter to an individual or company setting out its concerns. Although such letters have no legal status, they can be treated as a warning from the MCA that they are aware of potential operations which breach the legislation. Furthermore, these notifications are used as evidence of previous enforcement history when considering whether to commence a prosecution.

Simple Caution

A caution is largely used by the MCA for low level first time offending where there has been an admission of guilt and the offender accepts the caution. Therefore, cautions tend not to be used for serious offending. The MCA retain records of cautions and will bring these to the attention of the Court if an offender is found guilty of another offence.

Inquiry into Fitness to hold a Certificate of Competency

The MCA also has the power to conduct an inquiry into the fitness of an officer to discharge their duties by reason of incompetence, misconduct, for serious negligence or any other reason[140]. Such an inquiry can take place instead of a prosecution or as a result of it. The outcome of an inquiry can lead to an officer's certificate being cancelled or suspended. Inquiries can also be held into the fitness or conduct of seaman other than officers if one is requested by the holder of the certificate if notification has been given to them that their certificate is to be suspended or cancelled.

140 *See* s.61 of above.

CHAPTER FIVE

PROCEEDINGS ON DETENTION OF A SHIP

Further powers held by the MCA include the ability to detain a vessel, forfeit a vessel and/or use the Proceeds of Crime Act 2002 to take any benefit acquired from unlawful behaviour arising from breaches of the maritime legislation.

Detention Notice

In certain circumstances the MCA have a power to detain a vessel. The power to detain a vessel can be found under s.284 of MSA. The power to detain a ship can be exercised by a navy or miliary officer, any officer of the Crown authorised by the Secretary of State, a customs and excuse officer and any British consular officer[141].

Therefore, an MCA officer has power to detain a vessel. In a notice of detention, it has a discretion to require a ship to remain in a particular place or instruct it to be moved to a particular berth or anchorage. With such a direction the notice of detention can specify circumstances relating to safety or the prevention of pollution in which the master may move his ship from that place, anchorage or berth[142].

141 *See* s.284(1) of above.

142 *See* s.284 (1A) of above.

If a notice of detention has been brought to the notice of the master, it is a criminal offence to fail to comply with the notice of detention and any direction within it. This includes when a ship proceeds to sea before it has been released by a competent authority[143]. The MCA can also prosecute an owner of the ship or any person who sends the ship to sea if they are party or privy to the offence. In addition, if an officer authorised to detain a ship or the surveyor of a ship is carried away without his consent and whilst exercising his duty, a further criminal offence can occur[144].

There are a number of reasons why a ship may be detained. If a ship is in a port in the UK or at sea in UK waters and it is considered to be 'dangerously unsafe' and therefore it is unfit to go on a voyage or remain at sea without there being a serious danger to human life, the MCA are likely to engage their power to detain that ship[145]. Reasons for an unsafe ship can include amongst other things a defective hull and/or machinery, undermanning, unsafe loading or any other matter affecting the safety of the ship.

A ship can also be detained if it fails to comply with the requirements of the ISM Code Regulations 2014 under regulation 14 or if it does not have appropriate certification, documentation under some of the pollution regulations[146] and there is a reasonable threat of harm to the marine environment.

---

143 *See* s.284(2) and (2A) of above.

144 *See* s.284 of above.

145 *See* s.94 and 95 of above.

146 *See* for example Merchant Shipping (Prevention of Oil Pollution) Regulations 2019, regulation 38 and Merchant Shipping (Prevention of Pollution from Noxious Liquid Substances in Bulk) Regulations 2018, regulation 34.

If the master of a vessel of owner disputes a detention notice the matter can be referred to an arbitrator to determine whether there was a valid basis for the detention of a dangerously unsafe vessel[147]. Arbitration is also the dispute resolution available for other maritime regulations including those related to safety and for pollution prevention.[148]

The MCA will usually inspect a vessel when it is detained. A list of foreign flagged detained vessels for any given year can be found on the MCA website as a matter of public record.

Proceeds of Crime Act 2002

The MCA often rely on the powers under Proceeds of Crime Act 2002 ('POCA') to recover benefits arising from criminal conduct for offences under maritime legislation. As with any set of criminal proceedings, the recovery of any criminal assets will commence after a conviction. In the MCA's 2024 to 2025 annual report, £175,000 monies were received under POCA.

---

[147] *See* s.96 of MSA.

[148] *See* Merchant Shipping (Port State Control) Regulations 2011, SI 2011/2601, regs 15, 16 (as amended) and Merchant Shipping (Life-Saving Appliances and Arrangements) Regulations 2020, SI 2020/501, reg 21 and reg 22 of Merchant Shipping (Prevention of Pollution by Sewage from Ships) Regulations 2020 SI 2020/60, reg 18 of Merchant Shipping (Prevention of Oil Pollution) Regulations 2019 SI 2019/42, Merchant Shipping (Prevention of Pollution from Noxious Liquid Substances in Bulk) Regulations 2018/68, regulation 22.

Future Maritime Powers

Maritime Civil Sanction

At present the MCA's enforcement powers are limited to warnings and criminal sanctions for offending behaviour and breaches of the maritime shipping legislation. However, in 2021, the MCA did explore the prospect of extending its power to enable it to impose civil sanctions. A consultation was opened in October 2021 to amend MSA to make powers available to the MCA to include the power to impose stop notices, fixed and variable monetary policies. Suggested fines were to range from £250 to £50,000 for breaches of the merchant shipping legislation. At the time writing this book, there has been no formal response to the consultation and therefore it is unclear whether this is approach is likely to be taken in the future.

Other changes

Seafarers Wages Act 2023

The RCIT have been heavily involved in issues relating to seafarer's wages and passenger rights over the years. With the Seafarers Wages Act 2023, the key objective is to protect and improve remuneration for seafarers who have close ties with the UK. This will require a harbour authority to ask the operator of a service who enters its harbour 120 times or more a year for a declaration that confirms that seafarers who do not normally qualify for the national minimum wage are being paid the equivalent of that rate when working in UK territorial waters. The MCA will be given enforcement powers under the Act in respect of:

a. a harbour authority who does not request an equivalence declaration when they have reason to believe that a ship providing service will call at its harbour at least 120 times; or

b. for operators who act inconsistently with a declaration or give declaration which is false or misleading.

The Seafarers' Wages Regulations 2024 implements the Seafarers Wages Act 2023.

Public Office (Accountability) Bill

The Government's introduction of 'Hillsborough Law'[149] through the Public Office (Accountability) Bill will place duties on all public authorities and officials to act with candour, transparency and frankness. As a public authority responsible for maritime safety, the MCA will face the same duties under the Bill like any other authority such as the police, local governments and NHS bodies. The Bill also creates a legal duty of candour and assistance on authorities and officials at inquires, inquests and other investigations. This includes full disclosure of evidence whether it favours the public authority or not and there will be criminal sanctions for non-compliance. There will also be a duty to promote and maintain ethical conduct and two statutory offences will be created in respect of the public authority and officials who mislead the public. Provision is also being made for persons to participate at inquiries and investigations where the conduct of a public authority may be in question.

The MCA are regularly involved in inquests as HMCG is the lead maritime search and rescue emergency service. Furthermore, it fully co-operated in the recent Cranston Inquiry[150]. Therefore, it is unlikely

149 *See* https://bills.parliament.uk/bills/4019.

150 See https://www.gov.uk/government/publications/the-report-of-the-cranston-inquiry/the-cranston-inquiry-report-executive-summary.

that the new Bill will have a significant impact on the role that the MCA currently plays in inquests, inquiries and other investigations.

GLOSSARY

Aft The area toward the stern of the boat

Beam Width of boat measured at its widest point

Bow Front part of vessel

Bulbous Bow The protruding bulb shaped structure at the bow (or front) of a ship below the waterline

Chines Angle or line where the bottom of a vessel's hull meets the side

Cleat Metal fitting upon which rope can be fastened

Console Where the controls are located including steering, ignition, radio and other electronic devices

Deck Permanent horizontal covering over hull or compartment of a ship or boat (also known as the outside floor of the vessel)

Draft The distance between the waterline and keel of a boat

Engine Room Part of vessel where engine housed

Forecastle Forward part of ship's upper deck at bow. Traditionally used as crew's living quarters

Freeboard	The vertical distance between the waterline and main deck of a vessel
Funnel	Chimney or smokestack on a ship to expel exhaust gases, smoke and steam
Gunwhale	upper edge of vessel's side (*pronounced "gunnel"*)
Hull	body of a boat
Keel	A vessel's backbone which is the lowest point of a vessel's hull
Port	Left side of a vessel
Propeller	Rotates and powers a boat forward or backward
Rudder	Flat piece of wood or metal at the back of a boat or ship used for steering and maneuvering a vessel
Starboard	Right side of a vessel
Stern	Rear of a vessel
Superstructure	Section of vessel constructed on and above the upper or main deck of a vessel
Transom	A thick flat or slightly curved structural surface of the vessel that forms the stern of the boat
Waterline	The point at which the vessel sits in the water, i.e. the intersection of a boat's hull and the water's surface

Windshield	Screen located at the front of vessel to protect passengers from wind, sea spray and debris

MORE BOOKS BY LAW BRIEF PUBLISHING

A selection of our other titles available now:-

'A Practical Guide to Probation Breaches and Other Applications' by Mark Thomas
'A Practical Guide to Remarriage and Divorce' by Cordelia Williams & Claire Howard
'A Practical Guide to Privacy, Transparency, Reporting Restrictions and Closed Proceedings in the Court of Protection' by Laura Mannering
'Beaumont on Barristers – A Guide to Defending Disciplinary Proceedings (Second Edition)' by Marc Beaumont
'A Practical Guide to Payments for Environmental Services' by Ben Sharples
'A Practical Guide to the Law of Pregnancy and Maternity at Work' by Rebecca Thomas
'A Practical Guide to Redundancy – Second Edition' by Philip Hyland & Collette Moore
'A Practical Guide to International Issues for Scottish Family Lawyers' by Susie Mountain, Donna McKay, Ken MacDonald
'A Practical Guide to the Law on Deprivation of Liberty' by Ben Troke
'A Practical Guide to Rights over Airspace and Subsoil – Second Edition' by Daniel Gatty
'A Practical Guide to the Law in Relation to Inquests' by Ramya Nagesh
'A Practical Guide to the Construction and Rectification of Wills and Trust Instruments (Second Edition)' by Edward Hewitt
'A Practical Guide to Data Protection in Social Housing' by Clare Paterson
'A Practical Guide to Spousal Maintenance – Second Edition' by Liz Cowell
'A Practical Guide to International Parental Child Abduction Law (England and Wales)' by Dr Onyója Momoh
'A Practical Guide to Deprivation of British Citizenship' by Sean Ell
'A Practical Guide to Commercial Property Service Charges' by Rachel Garton
'A Practical Guide to Clinical Negligence – Third Edition' by Geoffrey Simpson-Scott (Geoff)
'A Practical Guide to the Rights of Grandparents in Children Proceedings – Second Edition' by Stuart Barlow

'The Electronic Communications Code: A Practical Guide – Second Edition' by Kerry Bretherton KC, James Castle, Mark Loveday
'A Practical Guide to the Independent School Standards – September 2023 Edition' by Sarah McKimm
'A Practical Guide to Estate Administration and Crypto Assets' by Richard Marshall
'A Practical Guide to Parental Alienation in Private and Public Law Children Cases' by Sam King QC & Frankie Shama
'Contested Heritage – Removing Art from Land and Historic Buildings' by Richard Harwood QC, Catherine Dobson, David Sawtell
'The Limits of Separate Legal Personality: When Those Running a Company Can Be Held Personally Liable for Losses Caused to Third Parties Outside of the Company' by Dr Mike Wilkinson
'A Practical Guide to Transgender Law' by Robin Moira White & Nicola Newbegin
'A Practical Guide to 'Stranded Spouses' in Family Law' by Mani Singh Basi
'A Practical Guide to Residential Freehold Conveyancing' by Lorraine Richardson
'A Practical Guide to Pensions on Divorce for Lawyers' by Bryan Scant
'A Practical Guide to Challenging Sham Marriage Allegations in Immigration Law' by Priya Solanki
'A Practical Guide to Digital Communications Evidence in Criminal Law' by Sam Willis
'A Practical Guide to Legal Rights in Scotland' by Sarah-Jane Macdonald
'A Practical Guide to New Build Conveyancing' by Paul Sams & Rebecca East
'A Practical Guide to Inherited Wealth on Divorce' by Hayley Trim
'A Practical Guide to Practice Direction 12J and Domestic Abuse in Private Law Children Proceedings' by Rebecca Cross & Malvika Jaganmohan
'A Practical Guide to Confiscation and Restraint' by Narita Bahra QC, John Carl Townsend, David Winch
'A Practical Guide to the Law of Forests in Scotland' by Philip Buchan
'A Practical Guide to Health and Medical Cases in Immigration Law' by Rebecca Chapman & Miranda Butler
'A Practical Guide to Bad Character Evidence for Criminal Practitioners by Aparna Rao
'A Practical Guide to Extradition Law post-Brexit' by Myles Grandison et al
'A Practical Guide to Hoarding and Mental Health for Housing Lawyers' by Rachel Coyle

'Stephens on Contractual Indemnities' by Richard Stephens
'A Practical Guide to the EU Succession Regulation' by Richard Frimston
'A Practical Guide to Solicitor and Client Costs – Second Edition' by Robin Dunne
'Constructive Dismissal – Practice Pointers and Principles' by Benjimin Burgher
'A Practical Guide to Religion and Belief Discrimination Claims in the Workplace' by Kashif Ali
'A Practical Guide to the Law of Medical Treatment Decisions' by Ben Troke
'Fundamental Dishonesty and QOCS in Personal Injury Proceedings: Law and Practice' by Jake Rowley
'A Practical Guide to the Law in Relation to School Exclusions' by Charlotte Hadfield & Alice de Coverley
'A Practical Guide to Divorce for the Silver Separators' by Karin Walker
'The Right to be Forgotten – The Law and Practical Issues' by Melissa Stock
'A Practical Guide to Planning Law and Rights of Way in National Parks, the Broads and AONBs' by James Maurici QC, James Neill et al
'A Practical Guide to Election Law' by Tom Tabori
'A Practical Guide to the Law in Relation to Surrogacy' by Andrew Powell
'A Practical Guide to Claims Arising from Fatal Accidents – Second Edition' by James Patience
'A Practical Guide to Asbestos Claims' by Jonathan Owen & Gareth McAloon
'A Practical Guide to Stamp Duty Land Tax in England and Northern Ireland' by Suzanne O'Hara
'A Practical Guide to the Law of Farming Partnerships' by Philip Whitcomb
'A Practical Guide to the Law of Unlawful Eviction and Harassment – Second Edition' by Stephanie Lovegrove
'A Practical Guide to Costs in Personal Injury Claims – Second Edition' by Matthew Hoe
'A Practical Guide to the General Data Protection Regulation (GDPR) – Second Edition' by Keith Markham
'A Practical Guide to Working with Litigants in Person and McKenzie Friends in Family Cases' by Stuart Barlow
'Protecting Unregistered Brands: A Practical Guide to the Law of Passing Off' by Lorna Brazell
'A Practical Guide to Secondary Liability and Joint Enterprise Post-Jogee' by Joanne Cecil & James Mehigan

'A Practical Guide to the Pre-Action RTA Claims Protocol for Personal Injury Lawyers' by Antonia Ford

'A Practical Guide to Neighbour Disputes and the Law' by Alexander Walsh

'A Practical Guide to Coercive Control for Legal Practitioners and Victims' by Rachel Horman

'A Practical Guide to the Law of Driverless Cars – Second Edition'

by Alex Glassbrook, Emma Northey & Scarlett Milligan

'A Practical Guide to TOLATA Claims' by Greg Williams

'A Practical Guide to Elderly Law – Second Edition' by Justin Patten

'A Practical Guide to Responding to Housing Disrepair and Unfitness Claims' by Iain Wightwick

'A Practical Guide to the Law of Bullying and Harassment in the Workplace' by Philip Hyland

'How to Be a Freelance Solicitor: A Practical Guide to the SRA-Regulated Freelance Solicitor Model' by Paul Bennett

'A Practical Guide to Prison Injury Claims' by Malcolm Johnson

'A Practical Guide to Advising Clients at the Police Station' by Colin Stephen McKeown-Beaumont

'A Practical Guide to Antisocial Behaviour Injunctions – Second Edition' by Iain Wightwick

'Practical Mediation: A Guide for Mediators, Advocates, Advisers, Lawyers, and Students in Civil, Commercial, Business, Property, Workplace, and Employment Cases' by Jonathan Dingle with John Sephton

'The Mini-Pupillage Workbook' by David Boyle

'A Practical Guide to Crofting Law' by Brian Inkster

'A Practical Guide to the Law of Domain Names and Cybersquatting' by Andrew Clemson

'A Practical Guide to the Law of Gender Pay Gap Reporting' by Harini Iyengar

'NHS Whistleblowing and the Law' by Joseph England

'Employment Law and the Gig Economy' by Nigel Mackay & Annie Powell

'A Practical Guide to Noise Induced Hearing Loss (NIHL) Claims' by Andrew Mckie, Ian Skeate, Gareth McAloon

'An Introduction to Beauty Negligence Claims – A Practical Guide for the Personal Injury Practitioner' by Greg Almond

'Intercompany Agreements for Transfer Pricing Compliance' by Paul Sutton

'Zen and the Art of Mediation' by Martin Plowman

'A Practical Guide to Adoption for Family Lawyers' by Graham Pegg

'A Practical Guide to Industrial Disease Claims' by Andrew Mckie & Ian Skeate
'A Practical Guide to Conducting a Sheriff Court Proof' by Andrew Stevenson
'A Practical Guide to Vicarious Liability' by Mariel Irvine
'A Practical Guide to Applications for Landlord's Consent and Variation of Leases' by Mark Shelton
'A Practical Guide to Relief from Sanctions Post-Mitchell and Denton' by Peter Causton
'A Practical Guide to Equity Release for Advisors' by Paul Sams
'A Practical Guide to Financial Services Claims' by Chris Hegarty
'A Practical Guide to Financial Ombudsman Service Claims' by Adam Temple & Robert Scrivenor
'A Practical Guide to Running Housing Disrepair and Cavity Wall Claims – Second Edition' by Andrew Mckie & Ian Skeate
'A Practical Guide to Holiday Sickness Claims – Second Edition' by Andrew Mckie & Ian Skeate
'Arguments and Tactics for Personal Injury and Clinical Negligence Claims' by Dorian Williams
'A Practical Guide to Drone Law' by Rufus Ballaster, Andrew Firman, Eleanor Clot
'On Experts: CPR35 for Lawyers and Experts' by David Boyle
'An Introduction to Personal Injury Law' by David Boyle

These books and more are available to order online direct from the publisher at www.lawbriefpublishing.com, where you can also read free sample chapters. For any queries, call us on 0844 587 2383 or email us at mail@lawbriefpublishing.com.

Our books are all generally in stock at www.amazon.co.uk with free next day delivery for Prime members, and at good legal bookshops such as Wildy & Sons.

We are regularly launching new books in our series of practical day-to-day practitioners' guides. Visit our website and join our free newsletter to be kept informed and to receive special offers, free chapters, etc.

You can also follow us on Twitter at www.twitter.com/lawbriefpub.

www.ingramcontent.com/pod-product-compliance
Lightning Source LLC
LaVergne TN
LVHW022303200926
848481LV00004B/1196
9781918241273